Testimonials for Uttam Shiralkar's previous book
'Smart surgeons Sharp decisions'

"Highly Commended book"
British Medical Association Awards 2011

"It is evident that only a surgeon, in having the necessary insight into a surgeon's functioning, could have written this book"
Journal of American Medical Association (JAMA)

"If intelligence is the ability to adapt in the light of experience, this book is a tool to help that process"
Australian & New Zealand Journal of Surgery

"This book is the key for surgeons who are looking for operating with maximal safety and achieving their best surgical performance"
Journal of College of Surgeons of Hong Kong

"This book should be a standard text"
Journal of the Royal Army Medical Corps

"This is an inspiring book. Great value for a surgeon at any stage of training, whether novice or part-time, retired"
The Journal of Laryngology & Otology

"The book offers an uncommon insight into the functioning of a surgeon."
Sujay Shad, Consultant Cardiac Surgeon, Delhi

"This book is about understanding that there is a great deal to being a surgeon, more than knowledge alone. It is a framework to get the best out of themselves every day through triumph and adversity"
J Earnshaw, Editor-in-chief, British Journal of Surgery

Cognitive Simulation

by

Uttam Shiralkar

MS, FRCS, MRCPsych

Published by
Surgical Psychology Publishing.
7 Brunswick Gate, Stourbridge. DY8 2QA UK
Tel: +44 (0)1562 884330
Web site : www.surgicalpsychology.com

First edition July 2013

ISBN: 978-0-9576801-0-4

Printed and bound in Great Britain by
Tyson Press, London

Dedication

To all those teachers who strive to make better surgeons for tomorrow.

Contents

About the author

Uttam Shiralkar qualified and worked as a surgeon for 15 years in the UK, India and USA, before entering the field of psychological medicine. A developing interest in psycho-oncology and the medical problems he faced after a car accident, were some of the reasons that contributed to this move.

While pursuing a career in psychological medicine, it became clear to him just how much of an impact a surgeon's psychology could have on clinical outcomes. He felt the need for surgeons to be made aware of this issue in a bid to address some of the shortcomings of the current system of surgical practice. Surgical colleagues with whom he shared the research findings from cognitive science, expressed a desire to find out more. What started as an informal chat with fellow surgeons became a formal course named 'Ergonomics for surgeons'. To share this knowledge on a wider level, he authored his first book titled 'Smart surgeons, sharp decisions'.

Currently, in addition to fulfilling his commitment as a consultant in the NHS, Uttam is actively involved in advising surgeons at various levels of their careers on a range of issues.

Foreword

The training of the next generation of surgeons is vital to maintain and advance surgical standards, helping them to use and pioneer the latest surgical techniques to save lives. With ever-increasing pressure on the time available to trainee surgeons to gain hands-on experience, it is critical that cutting-edge cognitive science is used to fully optimise surgical training.

While factual learning is an essential part of surgical training, the importance of acquiring technical surgical skills and developing proficiency in cognitive processing, for example in visualising the anatomical navigation of a surgical procedure, cannot be understated. Cognitive simulation develops these abilities using mental imagery to consolidate skills and knowledge into long lasting memories to aid surgeons perform complex surgery.

Drawing on the latest research on how cognitive simulation can be used in conjunction with traditional surgical training, Mr Uttam Shiralkar provides a timely and evidence-based guide to using cognitive simulation. Detailing practical examples into how to use such techniques to improve surgical performance, this book is a useful aid for surgeons at all career stages from trainee surgeons to senior consultants.

Professor Norman Williams
President of the Royal College of Surgeons of England

Acknowledgements

I would like to thank many of my friends for reviewing the draft and making valuable suggestions; especially, Mr John Watkinson, Mr Subodh Deshmukh, Mr Jason Green and Mrs. Anupama Shrotri. I would also like to thank Jackie Oliver for offering her input in editing and Gordon Shaw in designing the layout. I would like to thank Mr Robert Hamm for giving permission to use excerpts from his book 'surgical scripts' and Mr Milind Shrotri for providing cognitive simulation script. Thanks to Dr Ponkshe for organising the photographs.

Preface

A good quality surgery is said to have two key elements: safe judgment and good technical skills. My previous book 'Smart surgeon, sharp decisions' was about the first part: the judgement. As it turned out, this book was received rather well. The British Medical Association (BMA) awarded it a 'highly commended book' prize in 2011. The Journal of American Medical Association (JAMA) and the ANZ Journal of Surgery, among other journals, also had complimentary words to say. It was more than enough encouragement for me to set about writing about the second key element for successful surgery - the technical skills.

In this book, titled 'Cognitive Simulation', I want to focus on how important cognitive factors are and how surgeons can use them to improve operative skills. It aims to familiarise surgeons with the cognitive component of their operative performance and encourage them to view this concept with a critical eye albeit with an open mind. This book should help surgeons understand what cognitive simulation or, in popular terms, imagery, is.

Some surgeons may view the whole idea of imagery with suspicion, and even consider it to be esoteric. They may be of the opinion that hands-on experience with torrents of sweat from the brow is the only way to improve operative skills. Others may find it difficult to grasp the notion that mental training can improve a highly complex activity like surgical performance. Accordingly, this book appraises evidence-based techniques that readers can judge as to whether they have the potential to improve their performance. Understanding the theoretical basis behind cognitive simulation is what will help it to gain acceptance. For this reason, theory and research findings are provided after the introduction of the subject. The latter part of the book offers advice on how to put these concepts into practice.

The volume of literature on cognitive science, especially imagery, is growing rapidly. However it is available in areas other than surgery. Although visual information is indispensable for surgeons, there is little research from a surgical perspective. For a busy surgeon, gaining access to the literature on these topics is not easy. That being the case, there is an evident need for this kind of book aimed specifically at surgeons.

While this book is a guide to the art of skill acquisition, it is also designed to "help to fill in the pieces", and to pinpoint what is lacking in the current approach to help surgeons enhance their skills. It is no coincidence that experienced surgeons may find they already know some of the techniques mentioned in this book. In fact, those surgeons who have learnt through experience, will have subconsciously applied some of the techniques mentioned in this book. However, those who study this book will henceforth consciously apply the process to achieve better results. By being conscious of what they have been doing automatically, they will be able to actively improve operative skills.

In writing a book that introduces a new concept in surgery, I hope to encourage surgeons in the academic field to take up the challenge of investigating cognitive simulation with more enthusiasm. At the same time, I want to give practising surgeons information that they can work with. I also want surgical trainers and trainees to be aware of how this could shorten the learning curve. Cognitive simulation is a fascinating process and we still have much to learn about it. I hope that this book will help surgeons use these techniques to the greatest effect in improving their performance.

Chapter 1

Surgical performance - Mind the gap

"Life is short, the art is long, opportunity fleeting, experience deplorable and judgment difficult." - Hippocrates

Is this first aphorism from the father of medicine still applicable to current surgical training? With the expansion of surgical knowledge and changes in the training system that are unable to deliver a satisfactory education, for trainees, "never before has life been so short, the art so long, opportunity so fleeting, experience so deplorable and judgment so difficult"! (1). A study published in 2012 that analysed opinions from surgical trainers and trainees in the UK is telling: only 5% of the respondents believed that surgical training is improving, while 8% refused to comment, 18% thought there was no difference and a huge majority, 69% to be precise, felt that surgical training standards had deteriorated (2).

Surgical training dates as far back as the dawn of medicine. Over time, simple traineeships amongst family or friends made way for organised establishments. The apprenticeship system brought forth leaders who established 'schools of surgery', and trial and error methods coalesced into valid techniques. However, the absence of a methodical attitude to the training of surgical skills has dogged most of the 20th century (3).

Good surgeons, as we know, possess two vital attributes, safe judgment and good technical skills. All surgeons are expected to have these qualities (4). No doubt surgical culture has evolved along this line of thought. However, there are concerns about how well surgical training achieves this. First, there have been concerns about the unstructured nature of training. Although training that relied on on-the-job, learning-by-doing has been used for decades, its flaws have become apparent over time.

Another concern is about the variability in technical ability. The technical skills among surgeons, especially of trainees, remain highly variable, even when one speaks of basic skills like handling tissues and instruments.

With the emergence of minimally invasive technologies, skills are becoming more complex, rather than less, causing further widening in the variability.

The shrinking of learning opportunities in the operating theatre is another cause for concern (5). The changing patterns of healthcare delivery, greater accountability and shorter working hours have reduced training opportunities even further. Monetary constraints have forced policy makers to re-evaluate training methods. The cost in terms of time required to groom trainees in operating room imposes a financial burden. An American study estimated the cost of time lost during operations owing to surgical resident's involvement, was about $47,970 over four years of training (6).

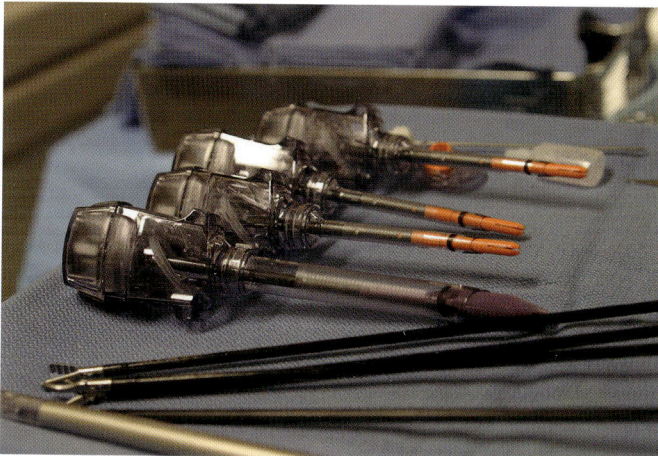

Laparoscopic techniques were introduced rather randomly and haphazardly in the early 1990's and they served to bring the need for a change in surgical skills training into greater focus. Cusheiri wrote: "Uncontrolled expansion of surgical endoscopic practice amounted to the biggest un-audited free-for-all in the history of surgery. In the past, surgical procedures have been introduced without evaluation and then later abandoned as either useless or frankly dangerous. However, those historic interventions received much less attention than laparoscopic procedures because they occurred on a smaller magnitude, in a less demanding era, and were driven by neither the expectations of patients nor commercial interests" (7).

The mushrooming developments in technology have pervaded the orbit of surgery profoundly. The minimally invasive surgical revolution has transformed the very practice of surgery. Image guided interventions in laparoscopic and arthroscopic surgery, natural orifice endoscopy and percutaneous intravascular procedures are becoming commonplace. These techniques require psychomotor skills in a manner not previously encountered. While minimally invasive surgery is a big boon to the patient, it is more demanding on the surgeon. Surgeons who were practising before the endoscopic era, have had to acquire new skills for performing these new procedures and to stay updated in their field. Endoscopic surgery has provided access to structures which in the past were unreachable without long incisions. However, it caused restrictions on surgeons as they have to operate from a distance, with elongated and difficult-to-control instruments. Similarly microsurgery has magnified and widened the choices of surgical treatments, as, lately, did robotics. Each advance in surgical technology has raised a distinctive interface between the operating surgeon and the patient's anatomy. The introduction of a new technique is followed by waves of learning curves, since new modalities change the dimensions of interface between the surgeon and the patient.

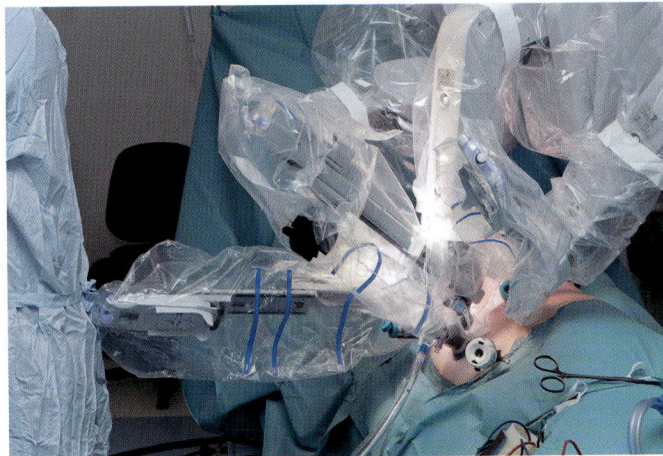

The downsides of the growing use of new technologies include, counter-intuitive instrumentation, two-dimensional viewing systems, an inadequate tactile feedback . These are the challenges that must be dealt with by a surgeon who intends to acquire new skills. The operating theatre, unfortunately, does not make for an environment conducive to acquiring new skills of this nature. In fact, a significantly reduced potential for learning in the theatre environment is what an inexperienced surgeon is likely to find. A surgeon whose skills are limited and who is not well versed with the operating team dynamics is bound to feel this sort of constraint even more acutely.

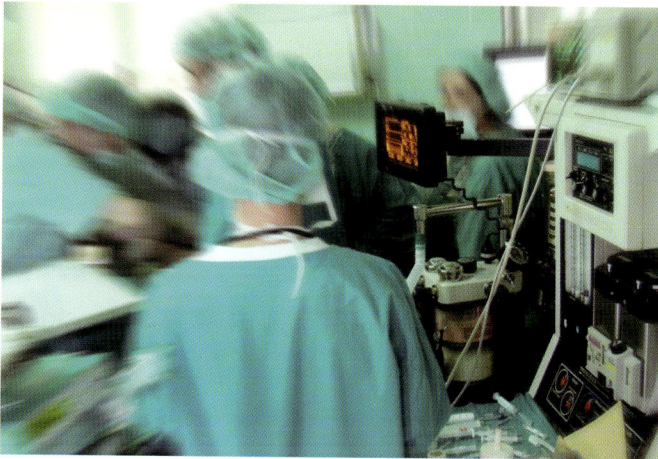

While it's true that an operating theatre is far from ideal for getting to grips with new found skills, it's also a fact that ways of training outside the operating theatre are not very conducive either. Being two-dimensional and devoid of physical interaction, books or DVDs are not suitable alternatives. This is where cadavers, live animals or bench models offer a viable option. However, each of these option has its benefits as well as limitations (8).

The cadavers provide a correct anatomic representation but the tissue characteristics may not be as representative as on a living patient. Besides, cadaver training is costly, entails only a one-time use for a specific procedure and they are in limited supply.

Live animals are an option that ensures an appropriate tissue texture but animal care is expensive. Along with the restrictions of one-time use and an anatomy not entirely representative of humans, it does not justify its worth. Animal welfare laws that vary from country to country restricting such procedures are also an inhibiting factor. More recently, possible contamination by Bovine Encephalopathy has raised another concern (9). Subsequently, dry laboratory models have become more popular. However, the general impression about the dry models is, they sacrifice fidelity for safety, availability, portability and reduced costs.

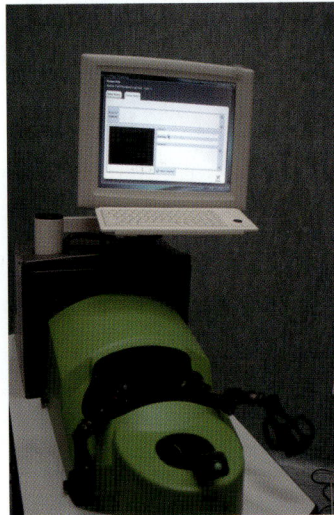

Upgraded computer technology has opened the door to more advanced and higher fidelity simulators. With the ability of their computers to create various scenarios, simulators have evolved from their primitive mannequin stage. Since simulators are potentially available round-the-clock, it is possible for training schedules to be flexible enough to allow other commitments and to be incorporated into other programs. A particularly intricate skill may be rehearsed many times over, until such time that the surgeon has overcome the problematic issues before operating on a patient. Simulators are known to facilitate adequate training for various other high-risk tasks where opportunity is limited by danger or impracticality. Like the flight simulators that allow airline pilots to be comprehensively instructed without endangering the lives of passengers, surgical simulators enable the acquisition of skills without posing a risk to the patient. Simulators also eliminate the risks of communicable disease to the surgeon imparted through sharps injury. In a nutshell, a simulator has the potential to save patients from trainees - and trainees from patients! (1)

Despite the benefits, the incorporation of simulation-based teaching in surgery has remained limited. Such training is typically confined to simulation centres, restricting their availability. Being more expensive than the low fidelity variety, the use of high fidelity models is not as widespread. Additionally, a closer scrutiny of simulation underlines the point that although methods vary, everything still depends on the physical rehearsal of surgical tasks. It is obvious that practice is crucial in gaining expertise in the surgical skills. Nevertheless, physical practice for multiple sessions at a simulation centre is an expensive proposition. It is also very time consuming and difficult to maintain over a period of time. Moreover, keeping to the recommended practice regimen is no guarantee of a surgeon's progress in skills.

The transferability of skills from a simulator is an important criterion in considering the benefits of simulators. Transferability reflects that skills acquired in one setting can be applied successfully in a different setting. The significant endorsement for simulators will be that their use results in improved performance in the operation theatre. The transferability of skills from simulators has been assessed in various studies – and some of the results are far from encouraging.

One such study, 'Does training laparoscopy skill in a virtual reality simulator improve surgical performance?' attempted to discover if practising on a simulator did translate into actual surgical performance - and the verdict was negative (10). Earlier research which showed that the use of simulators could familiarise surgeons with procedures, was found to be mostly confined to basic skills. What is more, invalidated tools were used to assess the skills transfer. The studies that showed the transfer of skills involving diverse tasks with the same simulator, however, bore no evidence that it improved performance in actual surgery (11).

Increased stress levels explains the incomplete transfer of simulator acquired skill to the operating room.
Surgery, 2010 (12).

This study aimed to evaluate the stress levels of surgeons during the transition from the simulator to the operating room, and the impact of the change in setting; on the performance.

Surgeons were randomly divided into intervention and control groups. After the training group attained competence in laparoscopic suturing, both groups were tested on a live porcine, laparoscopic Nissen fundoplication model. Their performance was judged by means of objective scores. Stress levels were monitored by recording beat-to-beat heart rate (BBHR) variability; at baseline; after reaching competency (for training group only) and in the operation theatre. It was noted that baseline simulator performance and heart rate variability were similar for both groups. After attaining simulator competency, the trained group showed a reduction in performance in the operation theatre and a rise in beat-to-beat heart rate. A similar but lower increase in beat-to-beat heart rate was seen in the control group compared to the study group. The investigators concluded "the increased beat-to-beat heart rate observed in the operation theatre that reflected stress and performance anxiety explained the incomplete transfer of simulator-acquired skill". This finding was similar to that of other studies that demonstrated that surgeons who achieved expert level performance on simulators did not perform at the same level in the operating room (13).

A different type of study (14) was conducted in the US to explore surgical residents' perceptions of different models of skills training. It involved senior general surgery residents and the use of four training tools.

1. Black box suturing model
2. Synthetic Nissen Fundoplication model
3. Virtual reality simulator suturing task
4. Porcine-Jejunostomy model

This was the participants' feedback after the workshop: the residents favoured the porcine model, followed by the Synthetic Nissen model and the black box suturing model respectively, with the virtual reality simulator at the bottom of the heap. In the participants' individual ratings, the animal model emerged the most popular, and the virtual reality simulator the most unpopular. Overall, the vote was not in favour of the virtual reality simulator. From an economic perspective, it cost $5 for Synthetic Nissen model, $12,000 per animal model, $18,000 for black box models and $125,000 for the virtual reality simulator. Isn't it interesting that the most expensive simulator was the least popular!

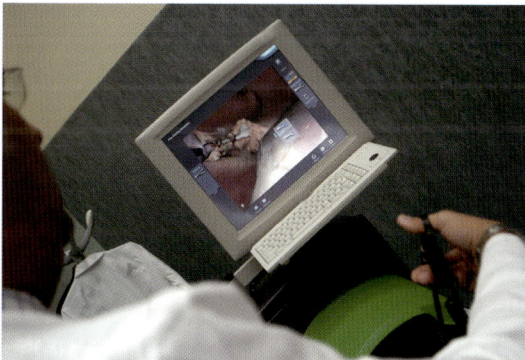

There are other drawbacks to using simulators. Procedural knowledge of surgical operations is best acquired by practising in the operating room atmosphere, with as many environmental similarities and limitations as possible in place. Current simulators have limitations in this regard. Another issue is that simulators are designed for set task and difficulty levels and trainees' individual experience levels are not taken into consideration. Some learners may feel overwhelmed by the complexity of the training task, while others may become bored or not challenged enough to progress. There is a crucial need therefore to take individual surgical skill and experience into account during training. Another point to note that, although the range of procedures being made available on simulators is on the rise, the variability is nowhere close to what occurs in real life surgical situations.

Industries such as aviation have long used simulation for training. There are some resonances between the flight deck and the operation theatre, especially in terms of team function and crisis management. Where these parallels break down however is in the dexterity, that is central to the work of a surgeon. Even in an emergency, an airline pilot does not have to perform the complex manoeuvers that a surgeon has to (15). The other telling difference between surgery and aviation is that in surgery every patient is unique and different in their presentation or anatomy, while the variations in airliners are limited and pilots know the variations explicitly, before taking to the skies. For this and other reasons mentioned earlier, surgeons cannot blindly adopt simulation technology from aviation despite some parallels between the two fields.

In zeroing in on the better way to learn surgical skills, we seem not to be taking advantage of what sectors other than aviation already know about acquiring skills. Malcolm Gladwell in his article on 'Performance' says that success in a skilled profession like surgery depends on three characteristics (16). The first is an individual ability, which Gladwell asserts, you either have or you don't. There is very little that can be done to nurture it. The second characteristic is practice. In contrast to the first characteristic, this one can be improved by individual efforts. The third characteristic, acknowledged by elite performers in various fields but never mentioned in the context of surgery, is imagination. Imagination, or the ability to improvise and to cope with novel situations, comes about through vision. Vision is seeing a possibility where others see none. Developing such a virtue entails not just experience but a certain orientation.

The application of 'imagination' to surgical skills is an esoteric art. Who would think of a connection between video games and surgical skills? A study (17) published in the Archives of Surgery discovered that surgeons who played video games at least three hours a week made 37% fewer errors, were 27% faster and performed 42% better than their non-playing colleagues. 3 surgeons, 21 trainees and 12 qualified surgeons from General Surgery, Urology and Obstetrics and Gynaecology, participated in this experiment. The surgeons among the top third in video gaming skills made 47% fewer errors and performed 39% faster than the other surgeons. The past and current amounts of play and video games skills were linked to speedier and more efficient performance. The conclusion was that surgeons who played video games are quicker and more accurate. Speed and accuracy do not usually go hand in hand in surgery, which makes these results all the more interesting. These results encouraged another group to investigate whether pre-planned training in video games could improve surgical performance (18). They explored if deliberate training in video games could improve performance on surgical simulators. The participants were instructed to systematically train on video games at home for 30 minutes a day, for five weeks. At the end of the training the researchers found that systematic video game training did in fact improve performance on the simulator. They also established the previous findings that "prior video game experience is positively correlated with performance in simulators. Overall, the potential of video games as training tools to enhance the acquisition of technical skills proved significant".

Such imaginative approaches highlight the need for other avenues to be explored to upgrade current training methods in surgery. In this regard, Kirk stated: "Recent changes in practice and organisation of surgery make it even more important to focus attention on acquisition of operative skills... by whichever possible means" (19). How far does the imagination need to be stretched to find the necessary solutions? Not too far. Indeed, it is seen that the solutions could be found very close to the surgeon: in the surgeon's mind itself.

Surgeons' cognition at the time of performing a procedure has been studied, especially in relation to cases that threw up complications. A study applied cognitive concepts in an attempt to understand surgical complications of bile duct injuries (BDI) in laparoscopic cholecystectomy (LC) (20).

This study analysed technical complications in greater depth by integrating the findings of videotaped operations, operative notes and concepts from

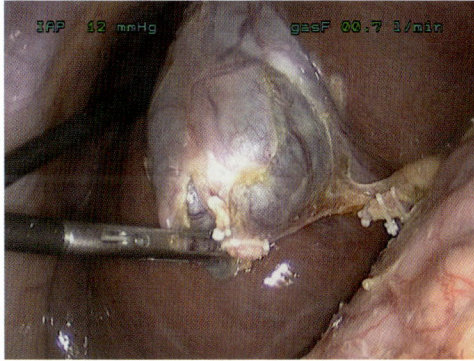

cognitive science. The authors scrutinised bile duct injuries in 252 cases of laparoscopic procedures. They did this study from the perspective of cognitive science relating to visual perception and human error. In every case, it was found that a surgeon had performed the procedure with an acceptable level of skill. The fault lay not in the actions but in misperceptions. The videos showed that the common bile duct (CBD) became prominent "as traction was applied on the gall bladder at the beginning of the procedure. The structural relationship between the bile duct and the gall bladder reflected the surgeon's mental model of the relationship between the cystic duct and the gall bladder. The illusion being convincing was believed by the surgeon as a fact".

In case of laparoscopic procedure, like any other surgery, the visual perception provides the main information regarding the gall bladder and adjacent tissues. In general the information from sensory organs is initially handled in the subconscious, after which conscious judgments are made about the movements. Unwanted outcomes could occur due to mistakes at any stage in the process. However, as this study showed, complications like laparoscopic bile duct injuries are predominantly an effect of misperception at subconscious level, and not due to deficiencies in the manual skill.

Cognitive pills for cognitive ills' a saying goes, and surgeons have used their imagination to devise cognitive solutions to address this cognitive problem of misperception. An evaluation of 34 patients of bile duct injury confirmed that misidentification of biliary anatomy was the main reason for injury, which it was deduced, occurs due to spatial disorientation, similar to navigation errors in aviation. These surgeons, thanks to their imagination, then adopted the principles used in navigation to solve the problem. Error prevention approaches extrapolated from aviation and naval fields were adapted. These adapted plans were applied in 2000 successive laparoscopic cholecystectomy procedures – and not a single injury occurred in any of the 2000 operations! (21).

Navigation principles applied in laparoscopic cholecystectomy

Start from a fixed point – The conventional secure initial point in open procedure is the fundus of the gall bladder. The fundus first technique is hard to apply in laparoscopic cholecystectomy (LC) due to the lack of traction on the liver after the fundus is mobilised. A substitute reference point to help the initiation of dissection is Rouvière's Circus, a cleft in the liver that can be seen to the right of the hilum, allowing the recognition of the location of the sulcus in 90% of patients.

Know where you are at all times – This is accomplished by a methodical assessment of the intra-hepatic surgical field, and it involves loosening the traction on the gall bladder and cystic duct, withdrawing the camera which will offer a large field of view and an inspection of the general relationship in the hepato-biliary triangle, confirmed with assisting surgeon.

The clearing bearing – This idea is extrapolated from a method used in coastline navigation to escape shallow water. A comparable principle can be applied for the dissection of the hepato-biliary triangle. Following the cut of the peritoneum in the safe triangle, signposted by Rouvière's sulcus, dissection is continued superiorly in the gall bladder fossa. This is done at adequate distance to open the hepato-biliary triangle fully, therefore confirming that any hilar duct structures are circumvented ('cleared' in naval vocabulary).

Another attempt to use cognitive methods to improve surgical performance evaluated whether orientation strategies could be imparted to surgeons to improve their performance. Thirty medical students participated, with half of them randomly assigned to a tutorial on orientation strategies at specific steps of the procedure, and the other half to a control group without any training. The intervention involved precise orientation plans used in four steps of the operation. For every step of the procedure, a video showed four aspects (22).

1. Regions of interest (ROIs) to be identified along with their importance: the best region of interest to be used as an 'anchor organ'
2. Other important organs, to be identified during each stage of operation
3. Regions of interest that should be used to distinguish orientation when related to other ROIs
4. Appropriate gaze fixation sequences associated with a successful reorientation

(It may be difficult to understand the significance of these steps without knowing the details of the study).

The results of this study showed that compared to the control group the intervention group became considerably more skilled in orientating the steps of the procedure. Training in orientation strategies enhanced performance significantly, with some reaching the equivalence of a surgeon with a long experience. These results could be extrapolated to surgeons who perform below average and they would to benefit from these cognitive interventions.

This type of training in cognitive skills is shown to be durable and the impact of training is seen to have lasting impact (23).

It is apparent therefore that for surgical skills, the axiom 'see one, do one, teach one' no longer suffices. Completing a surgical training program does not mean a certification in skill competence. Lectures, demonstrations, laboratory practice and simulation centres all have their benefits, but efficient methods with proven long-term effectiveness are hard to find. Even more rare are methods that ensure the transfer of skills to real world encounters. There still exist misapprehensions about skill learning such as, 'people learn in more or less similar ways'; 'knowledge lasts once learned', and 'individuals have the ability to integrate knowledge'. Learning surgical skills would be far easier if these beliefs were true. But it is not so. People learn in different ways, and an awareness of individual learning styles and capabilities is indispensable if we are to avert unwanted consequences. An imaginative approach will surely go a long way in dealing with these issues.

Can one cross over disciplines, and borrow the methodology of skill acquisition from sports? In sports, complex and unusual movements are learned to a high degree of proficiency (24). Similarly a surgeon's subtle movements are not part of the individual's usual range of movements. So, the requirements of the unusual movements are akin to the ones sportsmen encounter. The perfecting of complex manoeuvring is the aim in surgery, one that is common to professional sport. Given such common ground, it seems logical to syndicate surgery and sports science in an inter-disciplinary manner.

A surgeon can also be regarded as a performer, like a musician. Training and practice using a musical performance model, specifically, keyboard playing within a small chamber ensemble, shows an illuminating parallel to surgery. Like surgeons, solo keyboard players require high levels of digital precision and bi-manual co-ordination. Playing music in an ensemble is similar to surgery, which imposes demands such as the need to process complex information at high speeds and integrate it under pressure. It is possible then that diverse fields like sports, music and surgery could be considered to have similar issues to consider in improving performance.

Finally, it seems that in the context of surgical performance, there are gaps at various levels. Gaps exists between the quality of performance that the surgeon aims for, and the quality that is achieved in reality. There also exist gaps in ideal training methods and what is currently in use. The quality of skills among different surgeons shows wide gaps although they all have a similar experience. The point is, to improve the performance, these gaps between what is ideal and what actually exists must be taken into account. Not only do we need to mind the gaps, we must acknowledge that to close these gaps, our own 'mind' can be of immense help.

Key points

■ The conventional 'see one, do one, teach one' method of teaching is unsuitable in the current climate of surgical practice.

■ The introduction of new technology, expanding knowledge, increased accountability and reduced work experience has driven changes in surgical skills learning.

■ There are significant limitations in existing alternative surgical skill training methods.

■ Novel ideas are needed to bridge the gap between the existing and expected quality of skill training.

■ Surgeons need to adopt appropriate ideas from other performing disciplines.

■ Cognitive techniques have great potential in improving surgical performance.

Chapter 2

Anatomy of the surgical performance

"A surgeon should be youthful with a strong and steady hand which never trembles, and ready to use both hands with vision sharp and clear and spirit undaunted; filled with pity, so that he wishes to cure his patient, yet is not moved by his cries, to go too fast or cut less than is necessary; but he does everything just as if the cries of pain cause him no emotion." - Celsus,

First century medical encyclopedist

This first century description of the competent surgeon, still seems to be valid. Surgeons evaluate themselves by the barometer of operative skills. The halo effect from the perception that a surgeon has 'hands of stone' will certainly overshadow all the other good attributes he may possess. Technical skill is all-important for a surgeon. The technically astute have better mortality and morbidity outcomes, a valuable asset in the face of ever more knowledgeable patients. A surgeon in the course of his professional life, besides acquiring new skills, refines existing ones for greater efficiency.

It is not possible to optimise performance without understanding what it entails. Surgical performance encompasses an infinite number and variety of skills but there are common elements inherent in all of them. Specifically, skills are all learned through the same modus operandi, the neuromuscular system. Their intricacies may vary but the executive process remains one and the same, the nervous system. The manner in which the brain learns and executes skills is universal, regardless of diverse surgical specialities. Therefore, by understanding skill formulation, and how the nervous system works, performance can be improved.

Be they simple or complex, to improve skills, practice is presumed to be necessary. Indeed, practice and dexterity go hand in hand. While some skills may be acquired in a jiffy, the mastery of other, more arduous ones could involve hours or even years of dedicated effort. The constant however is the need for practice. An expert is acutely aware of the importance of practice, knowing well that a lack of practice affects the ability to perform optimally.

No surprise, 'Practice makes perfect' is a motto surgeons have adhered to across generations.

Isn't it surprising then that even though practice is regarded as so vital in surgery, better ways of practicing has not been pursued with an appropriate fervour? Is it because the emphasis on 'what to practise' has caused us to ignore 'how to practise'? Change, we must. Imagine, if it were possible for a surgeon to achieve expertise in absolutely any procedure within a very short period of time. Or acquire skills of the highest calibre. Or, for that matter, get a 'talent code' for 'gifted hands'. "It is not impossible if one realises that the secret of talent lies in perfecting the art of practice!", as one expert surgeon proclaims.

Scientists who study skill acquisition have observed sportsmen and musicians. These performers invest long hours in practising their actions. Permanent patterns of skilled behaviour are seen in elite professionals from these fields. Closer scrutiny reveals that in addition to visible practice, the elites also take recourse to covert rehearsals, which, it is now known, contribute significantly to their exalted quality of skills.

While learning a skill, we pay attention to the subcomponents of the skill. Sometimes however, skill acquisition occurs without paying attention to the components. Thus, two broad ways of learning skills are noted. One is analytical and the other is intuitive, also known as explicit and implicit. The intuitive learning does not involve conscious effort and needs minimal attention. This contrasts with analytical learning, where there is conscious effort to learn. Implicitly and explicitly acquired skills are stored in different parts of the nervous system. Explicit learning is stored in the premotor cortex and the implicit, in the sensorimotor cortex. How is this relevant to surgery? Let's talk about the pros and cons of verbal instructions given to a novice surgeon while learning a skill. Some people feel that if more verbal instructions are given, i.e.

more explicit learning, skill acquisition is better. On the other hand, others feel that the fewer the verbal instructions, i.e. more implicit learning, the better the quality (25). There is a view that an implicitly learned skill is less likely to fail under pressure than one that is explicitly acquired. As explicitly acquired skills involve and maintain conscious efforts to some extent, it is thought that during a time of crisis, the performer may not be able to maintain the same quality of skill. For example, in a study, golf players were assessed on their performance under conditions of induced anxiety, and it was found that there was a difference between the performance depending upon whether the skill was acquired implicitly or explicitly (26).

What is a skill?

At its most basic level, a skill is anything that one can learn to do. Even seemingly ordinary activities like driving or swimming are a skill. Learning a skill is a matter of turning things that one cannot do into the things that one can, in short, turning inabilities into abilities. A skill is nothing more than a collection of automated responses and actions. While learning a skill, we build and strengthen neural pathways. Master the art of building neural pathways, and we will also master the art of learning a skill.

In the initial phases when we practise a skill, we consciously make neurons fire one after another to achieve the movement. As these sequences fire repeatedly, the neural system begins to strengthen those pathways, which as they strengthen, reduce the need for conscious focus. This phenomenon is often described as developing a 'muscle memory'. To be precise, it is not only the muscles but the neuromuscular system as a whole that acquires the memory. The process of actions becoming habitual through repetition, is an important feature for learning a skill.

At a given time, the level of skill is what one is trained in, i.e. the unconscious part together with what the limited focus is directed at, i.e. the conscious part. These two processes work together during a performance. The capacity to store skill related information in the unconscious is unlimited, but the conscious part has a very limited quantum of focus. The path of improving skills is often obstructed by ignorance about using this limited focus effectively. What's more, incorrect practice may even result in regression of skills.

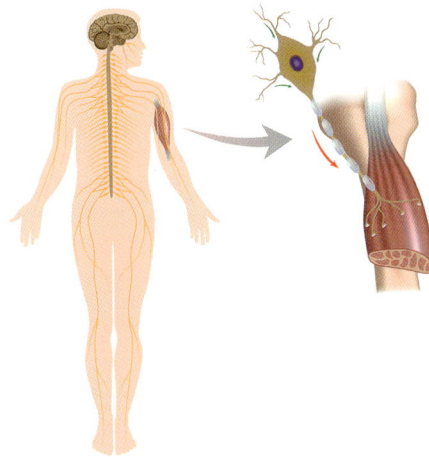

The distribution of attention allocation differs depending on the experience of the surgeon. When a novice is acquiring a new skill, he consumes the conscious focus to monitor what his hands are doing while trying to remember the steps of the operation. If there is an intra-operative event such as bleeding, he may not have the attentional resources available to take a note of it.

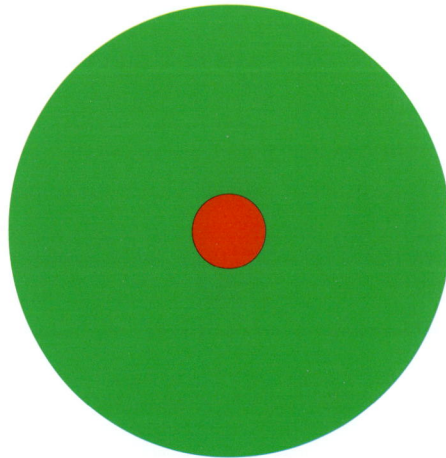

In the above picture, the green area represents the part of a skill that is performed unconsciously, whereas the red part represents the additional skill that can be achieved using conscious focus. Practice can be considered as using the focus to 'colour in' the red to green. However, for something to be converted to green, it must be placed in the red first. To do this efficiently, it is vital to know how skills develop.

Some surgeons describe surgical skill as a 'motor skill'. This description reflects a superficial understanding of the nature of the skill. Any skill, especially a surgical skill, is a psycho-motor process. What this means is that besides the visible motor aspect, there is a psychological or cognitive aspect of the skill. It is important to be aware of the cognitive factors that lie behind a surgeon's meticulous and subtle hand movements. The cognitive and motor parts are intertwined. This interdependence has an evolutionary foundation. Darwin stated that knowing the purpose it was designed for, helps in understanding the nervous system. In this regard, cognitive functions have evolved in line with motor skills, the evidence of which is the simultaneous development of higher cortical functions and dexterity of hand movements. How can dexterity be acquired without the direction from higher centres? The cognitive source behind the proficient movements of a surgeon must be taken into account.

The history of trying to improve technical skills from a psychomotor outlook can be found in a paper by Kopta, (27), who suggested a methodical assessment of psychomotor skills to find out how much skill learning has taken place. Another paper by Lippert (28) contended in favour of a formal psychomotor skills course for surgeons. From this side of the Atlantic, Prof. Ara Darzi has made concerted efforts to highlight the cognitive aspects of surgical skills.

Neuronal changes go hand in hand with the development of manual skills. Cortical matter grows in proportion to the use of the corresponding part of the limb. The capacity of the neurons to form possible connections is immense. It is not just a matter of the number of connections, but rather about the

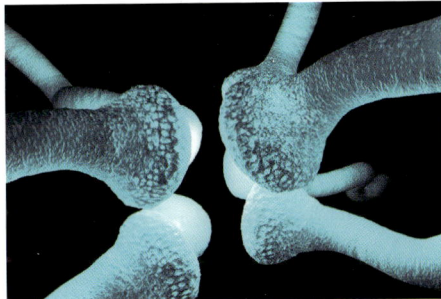

ability to grow more. A MRI study showed that the brain area controlling finger movement of musicians who played stringed instruments, had actually grown in size. This ability of the brain to grow is called 'neuro-plasticity', and it includes all possible mechanisms of neural reorganisations including synaptogenesis, sprouting of neurons, dendritic pruning, and postsynaptic thickening etc. The hands of elite racquet players show increased motor-evoked potential amplitude and a reduced cortical motor threshold (29). It is evident then that acquiring dexterity is accompanied by functional reorganisation in the brain.

Could variations in technical skills acquisition in surgery be explained by differences in cortical plasticity?

Annals of Surgery, 2008 (30)

Functional changes take place in the cerebrum of surgical trainees as they acquire surgical skills. It is seen that neuro-plasticity accompanies expertise development amongst surgeons. Actually, the 'surgical brain' may demonstrate an interesting example for studying plasticity due to the intricacies of the stimulus - surgery. Illuminating the neuro-cognitive process that underlines acquisition of skills may help in the training and selection of potential surgeons.

In this block design trial of surgical knot tying that included 62 participants of variable surgical experience, prefrontal activation was seen in trainees but not in experienced surgeons. This offers an illustration of cortical oxygenation difference between an expert and novice surgeon. The discrepancy in performance and attainment of surgical skills can be clarified by differences in cortical function and neuro-plasticity. These kind of studies may be of help in identifying a surgeon in need of assistance.

Novel and proficient movements of the same task have shown different cerebral activation in other studies as well (31). These structural changes seen in the nervous system are necessary for retention of a skill. However such 'hard wiring of neuronal circuits' creates difficulties to change once it has been coded in the nervous system (32). This is one reason why it is so difficult to rectify an incorrectly learned skill. Another problem due to neuronal coding occurs while deconstructing an automated task. We see this happening in the teaching of a complex skill to an oblivious learner. As a result of the coding, the explicit details of skills are not easily available for description.

Stages of skill learning

When we acquire a skill, the learning occurs in three stages, namely; the cognitive stage, the associative stage and an autonomous stage (33).

The cognitive stage involves understanding the task. In this phase, the learner seeks an explanation of the skill and observes the skill performed by others. In a surgical context, it entails conceptualisation of the skill, during which the indications, contra-indications, complications and basic technique of the procedure are understood. The importance of the cognitive stage is seen from the experiments that showed the trainees who were offered sufficient explanation of the technique were more likely to acquire the skill than those who did not have sufficient understanding (3).

A simple procedure like colonoscopy illustrates the practical aspects of the cognitive phase. During the cognitive phase of colonoscopy, the novice becomes familiar with the basic functions of the colonoscope, in addition to the anatomy of the large intestine. He is expected to be aware of concepts such as looping and paradoxical scope movements. The trainee should know and be able to describe how to counteract these difficulties, such as by applying pressure and reducing the length of the bowel.

A satisfactory cognitive phase is a necessary component in skills acquisition. Cognitive activities can be learned in a structured manner with the use of didactic sessions, case studies, videos and demonstrations. These instructional methods serve as a bridge to the second phase, which is the associative stage.

In the associative stage, skills distinctive to the task are applied to prevent ineffective actions. During this phase, the performer is able to comprehend and put into practice the mechanics of the skill and respond to the feedbacks. To use colonoscopy as example again, in this stage, the surgeon will be able to navigate through the straight sections of the colon and perhaps also be able to complete a relatively simple procedure. However, the performer may need feedback throughout and possibly assistance at some stages.

In the last stage of automation, the skills turn out to be automatic. One does not need to ponder over every stage or to count on outside clues. In this stage, the surgeon should be able to perform the task with speed, efficiency and precision. The skill undertaken needs minimal cognitive input, with the focus directed almost entirely towards refining the performance. The skill at this point is fluid, continuous and adaptive (34).

It must be noted that although these stages are mentioned discretely, in practice, at a particular stage of learning, all these stages may occur at the same time. Some aspects of the procedure may be in the cognitive stage while others may be in the stage of automation. For example, while learning to perform hysterectomy, the surgeon may be tying the knots automatically while making efforts in a cognitive stage to proceed to the next step.

The type of suggestions that benefit the progress of skills varies among the initial and final stages. During the early stages, the most important aspect for skill acquisition is perceptual understanding with consideration of spatial relations, and a grasp of the mechanical factors. However in the subsequent stages, actions involve pace, efficacy as well as accuracy. Although the three phases overlap and are not discrete, the value of the cognitive phase must not be underestimated. A trainee who has assisted in operations many times could yet be all at sea when performing the same operation for the first time on his own.

The neurological foundation of the stage of automation that underlines surgical proficiency, is the 'hot-wiring' of a plan of the performance into neural tracks. For this reason it is tough for senior surgeons to display the details of a procedure to trainees, even for something as simple as tying a surgical knot. The actions of an experienced surgeons are difficult to isolate, and complex manoeuvres acquired by observation may be challenging to break down into sections.

Measuring mental workload during the performance of advanced laparoscopic task (35).

Mental workload is a limited faculty and is in-demand when acquiring a new skill or carrying out complicated undertakings. Therefore measuring a surgeon's mental workload may indicate his expertise. This concept is frequently attributed to Abraham Maslow, although the model does not appear in his major works. The premise of this study was described as those surgeons who are expert in a skill are expected to have additional mental resources to handle an ancillary job, compared to surgeons who are inexperienced. In this study, participants performed standardised laparoscopic suturing on a bench-top model. 12 trainees and 9 experienced surgeons were asked to perform as many sutures as possible in six minutes. A nearby screen randomly showed 30 true visual signals among 90 false signals. Subjects were expected to recognise the true signals whilst they continued suturing. The Fundamentals of Laparoscopic Surgery (FLS) scoring scheme was used to assess the sutures. The secondary (visual detection) task was assessed by counting the frequency of overlooked true signals or counting in a false signal. The findings revealed that experts completed significantly more secure sutures than novices. The suture performance score was 50 +/- 20 for experts, significantly higher than for novices (29 +/- 10). The rate for detecting visual signals was also higher for experts. The authors concluded that repetition progresses to automaticity that lessens the mental workload and permits surgeons to have enough spare mental capacity to deal with an additional task. Visual recognition offers an easy and dependable method to evaluate mental workload and situation awareness abilities of surgeons during skills training. Also it serves as an indirect evaluation of expertise.

Phases of skill learning

There is another way to understand how we acquire a skill. According to this, skill acquisition goes through four 'phases' of competency. This concept is frequently attributed to Abraham Maslow, although the model does not appear in his major works.

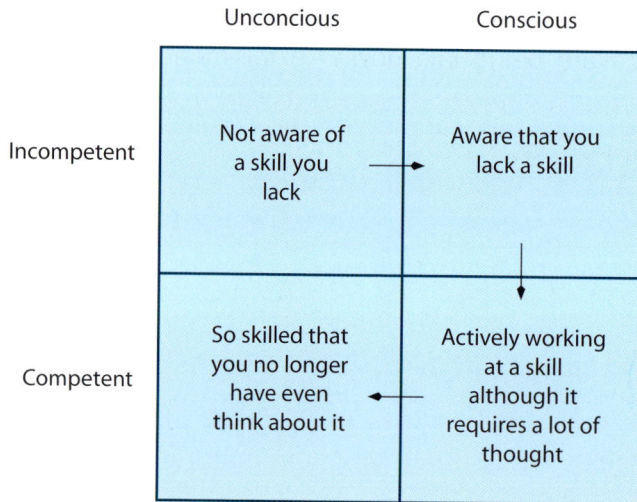

	Unconcious	Conscious
Incompetent	Not aware of a skill you lack	Aware that you lack a skill
Competent	So skilled that you no longer have even think about it	Actively working at a skill although it requires a lot of thought

1. Unconscious incompetency

This first phase is the inability to perform a skill. This could be either due to lack of knowledge, not knowing how, or due to a lack of insight – believing that one has the skill when in reality one does not. Transcending this phase involves developing an awareness of both what one is unable and able to do.

2. Conscious incompetency

In this phase one comes to realise not only what one is incapable of doing, but also why. There is also an awareness of the correct method. However, knowing 'why' does not guarantee the ability to actually perform.

3. Conscious competency

The third phase is defined by the ability to perform the skill. A surgeon can be technically proficient enough to do what he is called upon to, but this proficiency needs to function sub-consciously if he is to attend to other matters relevant to the performance.

4. Unconscious competency

Upon reaching this level, the neural pathways necessary for the performance are being laid down. In this final phase, a skill becomes automatic. At this stage a surgeon does everything in a correct manner without making conscious efforts.

Master surgeons operative teaching philosophies:
A qualitative analysis of parallels tolearning theory (36).

Leading surgeons use various principles of learning theory while imparting training. The purpose of this study was to recognise how master surgeons approach training. The study revealed that many of the themes that emerged from the surgeons paralleled the principles of learning theory. The key elements were; graduated responsibility, encouraging development of a mind set, fostering deliberate practice and deconstructing complicated tasks. Half of the respondent surgeons stressed that trainees are required to be sufficiently prepared before the operation so that they can learn effectively in the operating theatre. This idea of preparation equals the learning theory notion of developing a mental set, a process that prepares the mind to take in and organise new information. Preoperative preparation involves obtaining related information about the procedure to be performed.

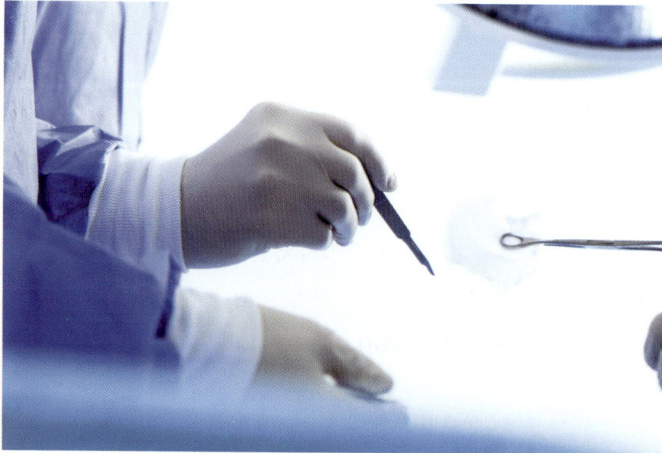

i^3

i cube

To derive the best from experience, certain strategies can be relied on to improve the quality of the practice. The i cube or the 3 'I's stand for Identification, Isolation and Improvisation.

Identification

The first step is to identify and obtain information about the desired skill. In a surgical context it may be a particular surgical procedure, or a specific step in a surgical procedure. This strategy centres around becoming aware of just what needs to be installed in the neuromuscular system. All a surgeon needs to do is to become aware of what is to be learnt and the correct way to do it. This can be achieved by pinpointing the difference between the current practice and the perfect way to execute the skill.

Isolation

The inability to isolate a particular part of a skill is a common problem among performers. By identification, a surgeon may know what he needs to do, but just knowledge does not grant the ability to perform to an acceptable standard. Since a learner's new skill has not permeated to an unconscious level, the matter being learned must be made small or handy enough to fit into the conscious mind. An isolation of the skill is what is necessary for that to happen.

We do come across people who may have performed a procedure many times and yet be unable to improve their skills, no matter how hard they try. This is partly due to the conscious mind being flooded with too much information. High error rates also indicate that the brain is being overloaded. Reducing the amount of data then is the key to isolation. The three categories of information that affect the performance are:

1. The complexity of the skill
2. The speed of acquisition of the skill
3. The level of perfection one intends to achieve.

The first aspect is simply the size of the skill to be mastered. Skills of higher levels have higher complexity and higher volumes of data. The second deals with how quickly a surgeon wishes to learn the procedure. The faster the speed, the greater is the data. Reducing the data in any one area will allow an increase in another. In other words, there is a scope for trade-offs between these three categories. We all know that one can cope with a new or complex skill if it is performed slowly or less fastidiously.

It must be remembered however that lowering the category of 'perfection' should be the least favoured option in a trade-off. Quick practice of a complex task with a low standard of competency will only reinforce that imperfection. However, slowing down or lowering the complexity while aiming steadfastly for perfection, will eventually allow an increase in both complexity and speed. Lowering the complexity or the speed too much may also make the goal too easy, non-stimulating and even boring to attain. This may not be as undesirable as trying to learn too much at once, but it certainly means that the learning process could be more efficient. So, just as being overwhelmed is not productive, being underwhelmed is no good either. Practice therefore should be at an appropriate level for the conscious mind to process.

Improvisation

The brain needs time to complete the learning process, to organise and store data in the unconscious. Adequate maturation is necessary for competency. Maturation also solidifies the basics of a skill that leads to more complicated stages. Sometimes a novice may be unable to get a procedure right for very long, and then out of the blue, his proficiency increases and he is able to perform the skill perfectly well. On the other hand, a surgeon despite weeks of not practising or not performing a procedure for years, delivers above average results. The process of neural maturation can explain both examples.

There are practical implications of the maturation process. Frequent practice sessions of short duration will produce greater results than less frequent but longer ones. Why? Because smaller practice sessions with intervals in between grant the time required for maturation. The same principle applies at a micro level with a single practice session: it is better to split up what is learnt and cycle through the modules rather than focus on one module for several hours at a time. Or one could work on something different for a short while and then return to the previous arduous module, which could get considerably easier the next time around.

Perceptual ability and surgical skills

Technological innovations have permitted surgeons to miniaturise their eyes to carry out microscopic procedures and lengthen their fingers to conduct endoscopic interventions that were unthinkable just a few years ago. However that does not mean that the need for dexterity has diminished. Not only has the need for dexterity remained high, in addition, there is a greater need for greater perceptual skills (37).

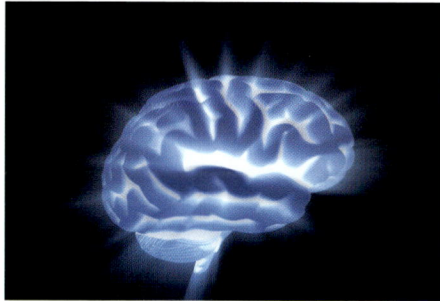

Surgical expertise involves a multi-sensory interaction of experience. It has been suggested that perceptual skills training should be incorporated into the surgical curriculum (38). One of the reasons for introducing perceptual skills is to develop efficient procedural knowledge. A surgeon who appears to know what to do, i.e. declarative knowledge, nonetheless, could be lacking in the skill to proceed, i.e. procedural knowledge. Handling surgical instruments competently and controlling hand movements is a vital ability, which relies on perceptual senses. Site-specific morbidity is directly linked to an incapability to correctly handle the instruments, which may be a result of perceptual problems. Trainees observing surgeons performing procedures within the time constraints find it difficult to perceive their perceptual aspects. It is possible that subtle procedural knowledge regarding hand motions and instrument control is difficult to spot and appreciate while the trainee is assisting in a demanding procedure. Subsequently, these methods of training are not the most helpful methods for surgeons to completely understand the necessary procedural knowledge.

Cognitive science emphasises the importance of perceptual information about the procedure without denying the importance of knowing the steps. For sure, practice *per se* has its place in the acquiring of skills, but the real benefit is in the information that the performer perceives while performing. Developing strategies to process and retain perceptual information does benefit the development of skills. The sensory information is processed and stored in the form of a mental model. The quality of this mental model determines the quality of performance. Understanding that surgical performance is a cognitive activity that involves the processing of perceptual information helps in advising surgeons how to develop strategies to process and retain this perceptual information effectively (39).

Richard Schmidt's 'schema theory' provides a framework to understand the importance of perceptual abilities in performance. He outlines four categories of information necessary for the execution of a skill: initial conditions; response specifications; sensory consequences, and response outcome (40).

1. Initial conditions - The initial conditions consist of the information received from various senses prior to an action. This may be proprioceptive information about the position of a hand or visual information that the patient is lying on the table under anaesthesia in a surgical position.

2. Response specifications - Since the motor program for generation of muscle commands is assumed to be rather general, the performer needs to specify detailed requirements before the movement can commence, such as stretching the skin with one hand and starting the incision with the other hand from point A to B.

3. Sensory consequences - This consists of the actual feedback received from the eyes, proprioceptors etc. For example, the completed incision from point A to point B, bleeding from the incision and the tissue exposed after the incision.

4. Response outcome - This arises from information the surgeon receives after the action and consists of knowledge and results of his action.

The application of this theory to learn a surgical skill can be seen in the following example.

A novice surgeon making a skin incision for the first time may not have previously acquired information regarding the response specification, the sensory consequences, and response outcome. This means that he does not know how much pressure he should apply to make a correct incision. Also he is unaware of what sensory feedback he should receive after he starts making a cut and what would be the response outcome when he has completed the incision. The result, more often than not, is the application of insufficient pressure on the scalpel and an incision of inadequate depth.

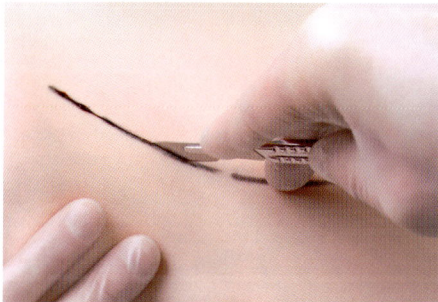

After the initial performance, information about each of the four categories is stored. This information can subsequently be used for the next performance. Each new performance provides information that helps refine subsequent movements. In the case of a novice surgeon making his subsequent incision, the sensory information on such factors as type of skin, thickness of subcutaneous fat, pressure applied to the scalpel, position of the hand and result obtained - is stored and will be used to plan the next incision correctly. Presumably, more pressure will be applied at that time and the trainee will store the information within each of the four categories that will be used for the following incisions. The stored information from the four categories described, not only helps in the performance of similar movements in future, but it also helps to generate a range of expected sensory consequences. In the case of an experienced surgeon performing a skin incision, this would consist of understanding the significance of the appearance of skin and its expected response to the application of a certain amount of pressure on the scalpel, such as thick versus thin skin, which is confirmed in the visual feedback of the scalpel cutting through the skin and the proprioceptive feedback received as the skin is incised (41).

How does understanding this theory help surgeons to improve? Let us revisit the novice surgeon making his first skin incision. In this example, for the sake of clarity only the pressure applied to the scalpel was considered. However, several other senses are involved in making an incision: such as the angle of the blade, the grip on the scalpel, the surgeon's posture, and so on. In reality all this happens at a subconscious level, but one can consciously focus on a particular aspect, and seek feedback on that component. The feedback should allow for analysis of the perceptual information received during the procedure. Feedback will be useful only if the learner internalises the comments by linking them to the sensory information. Thus, the learner will be able to adjust the data in the appropriate mental model and only then be able to correct the next performance. This can be achieved by guiding the trainee in the analysis of a performance. Apart from a formal educational setting, the surgeon can reflect on his performance himself and concentrate on specific features of the perceptual feedback.

The results of neuropsychological testing experiments on surgeons follow the principles elaborated on by Schmidt in his theory. Good perceptual abilities allow the learner to form a better model of the procedure, to predict the consequences of performance, and therefore to plan and adjust the movement with greater accuracy. The learner is also able to interpret more efficiently the feedbacks and will have a richer network of information regarding Schmidt's four categories.

Visuo-spatial skills in surgical performance

What specific perceptual skills influence surgical performance? A number of studies have shed light on the immense value of visuo-spatial skills in surgery. In one study surgical trainees underwent a battery of neuropsychological testing which included motor skills and visuo-spatial skills assessments (42). When the test results were compared with the surgical trainees' score of their skills during actual surgical procedures, the scores on the skills were found to be significantly correlated with visuo-spatial skills but not with motor abilities. Surgical performance which involves spatially complex procedures appears to be strongly related to a surgeon's performance on visual-spatial tests (43).

Visual-spatial ability and fMRI cortical activation in surgery residents.
American Journal of Surgery, 2007 (44).

In this study a group of surgical trainees underwent fMRI while they were responding to a visuo-spatial test Mental Rotation Test (MRT).

MRT is a validated test to evaluate individual visuo-spatial skills. When the participating surgeons were undergoing functional MRI, they were presented with either the MRT or a control task. The control task did not involve any visual-spatial testing. The findings identified cortical areas that have the greatest connection with MRT performance. Superior MRT performance was associated with larger activation in cortical areas associated with visual imagery and motion processing. These results imply that the difference in performance on spatially complex tasks containing imagery reveals diverse spatial problem solving approaches among surgeons. This variation, which was tested objectively in this study reflects the factors behind performance variation amongst surgeons.

What are visuo-spatial skills?

Visuo-spatial skills refer to the ability to visualise a three-dimensional situation using anatomical landmarks. An effective visuo-spatial ability facilitates a clear mental picture of the relationships between the landmarks. Thanks to this mental illustration, the surgeon can plan and execute the procedure with greater precision. An experienced surgeon continuously adapts executive routines to new situations, the adaptation evolves from one case to another. The dimensions of the wound, the distances between anatomic structures, the relative positions of landmarks, the amount of fatty tissue etc. may vary. The surgeon must perceive and recognise the differing conditions and adjust movements accordingly. The quality of performance depends on a surgeon's ability to build in his mind a model of the workspace - and this is where expertise relies on visuo-spatial skills. The quality of this representation depends on the interpretation made from the available visual information (45).

Since visuo-spatial ability is an ability to manipulate mental models of a visual and spatial nature, for clearer understanding let's consider the two aspects separately. The relationship between pure visualisation and surgical proficiency is well charted. Visualisation correlates with time on task for a number of surgical tasks, with the quality of surgery as measured by a rating scale and with the quality of surgery as measured by simulator outcomes. (46). That surgeons score higher on visualisation tests than a comparable sample from the general population, is also a fact (47).

Spatial relation is the ability to manipulate simple mental representations quickly. A number of studies have revealed a strong correlation between spatial ability tests and performance rating on a range of tasks in surgery (48). Spatial properties include location, movement, extent, shape, and connectivity. The surgeon needs to create a mental image of three-dimensional anatomy from the single dimension view or cross sections from X-ray, CT, MRI, or ultrasound images. Based on experience and anatomical understanding, he needs to devise a plan to gain exposure of relevant anatomical structures to get the expected results (49).

In minimally invasive surgery, surgeons rely on video images of the internal structures and use instruments restricted by a fulcrum at their passage through the incision. This calls for further mental transformation of the image and cautious preparation to overcome the restrictions. As mentioned earlier, learning surgery from books, videos, and CD ROM is difficult since they are not ideal media to train from a spatial perspective; being two-dimensional, the user cannot physically interact with them.

Problems in the spatial aspect of perceiving information during endoscopic surgery are seen due to handling of the camera. The surgeon may not have a direct control over the position of the endoscopic camera, and has to rely on the assistant to maintain the position. Sometimes unintentional rotation of the camera occurs that leads to disorientation and misinterpretation of position of the organs. Spatial discrepancies are also caused by misinterpretation of angular relationships if the entry points of instruments do not correspond with the optical axis of the endoscopic camera.

Results of experiments on spatial relations have correctly predicted performances of surgeons on microsurgical procedures (50). Spatial ability is a key predictor of performance in other surgical procedures as well. In one study, (51) investigators observed variations in performance as surgeons learned to use an angled laparoscope. In this experiment, novices took tests of spatial ability. After the baseline test they learned to use an angled laparoscope in a virtual environment for 12 sessions. Initial performances displayed significant variability amongst operators, with performance related to their differing spatial abilities. As learning progressed, inter-individual variability got reduced. However the correlation of the performance with spatial ability remained significant. These results indicate that the role of spatial ability remain vital even after a skill has been acquired.

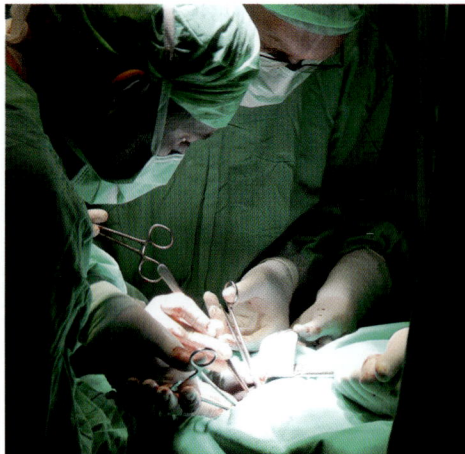

Observational learning

Observational learning is an important aspect of skill acquisition in surgery. Observation allows learners to acquire a mental 'blueprint' of the action intended.

Modelling surgical expertise for skill acquisition

The American Journal of Surgery (52).

In this study, trainee as well as expert surgeons performed inguinal hernia operations which were video recorded. Later the trainees in the experimental group were shown the procedures by split-screen technique. The split-screen display meant that the participants watched an expert surgeon on half of the monitor, while the other half of the monitor showed the trainee performing the same procedure. By simultaneously showing the video of two different skill levels, direct comparisons were made to appraise skills. This kind of comparison would not be available from watching a conventional video of just one performer. Split-screen viewing is helpful for skill learning as the observer watched and analysed two different levels of movements at the same time. This process complements cognitive modelling. Watching comparative performances in a single display stimulates dynamic processing of the skills. The results of this study showed distinct benefits for the experimental group as they required less time to complete the procedure and showed more economy of movements. An explanation for these results offered was recognising movement clues in the action whilst watching the expert's video helped the trainee to form a better mental model of movements and control. Concurrently, trainees equated their actions with the experts' actions in a split-screen display, getting precise feedback. Thus the intervention group experienced perceptual knowledge by observing the spatial and temporal relationships contained in the operation. Exposure to the perceptual information improved the actions for handling surgical instruments. It also improved the procedural knowledge.

How much time should a surgeon spend on observation and how much hands-on experience is necessary? The observation period allows the learner to concentrate fully on perceiving the procedure visually and spatially, to process this information and to build mental images. During hands-on practice or while performing a procedure, learners are unaware of many other stimuli due to reduced attention needed to acknowledge the stimuli. Observation and practice therefore are complementary ways of learning surgical skills.

To discover if there is was any advantage in using observational learning in combination with physical practice, Ashford et al (53) carried out a meta-analysis on 68 studies involving a range of skills. They confirmed that additional benefits occur when performers use observational learning in combination with physical practice, rather than physical practice alone. In another study, 55 participants were separated into three groups, an observational learning group, a mental practice group, the third being a combination of the two. It was found that the combined intervention of observing video clips and mental practice led to a greater improvement in performance than either observational learning or mental practice alone.

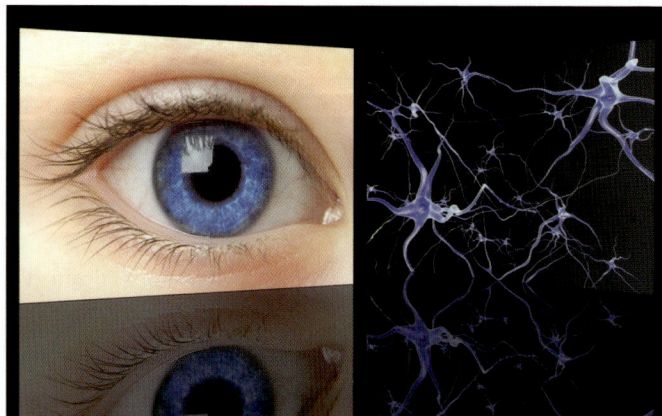

There are special types of neurons in the frontal cortex known as mirror neurons. These special neurons are activated not only when someone is performing an action, but also when they are is merely observing the action being performed (54). Imaging and neurophysiological studies have confirmed the presence of mirror neurons in premotor cortex and it is now known that they also play a role in imagery (55).

The quality of observational learning depends on the instructions the observer has given himself or somebody else has given him regarding how or what to observe in the procedure. A simple instruction like 'what to observe' significantly affect the mechanics of skill acquisition. Depending on whether the person is observing an action merely to recognise it or whether he is observing it with the intention to perform it himself, the nervous system responds differently. Decety's study (56) proved that the motor cortex is involved in observational learning only if participants intended to perform the action themselves. There seems to be a requirement 'to hold' the observed action within the motor areas, when the observer intends to perform the action in the future. This explains the difference amongst surgeons attending a live surgery by a renowned surgeon: those who observe with the intention of performing the procedure themselves at a later date will benefit more from observing live surgery than those who observe passively just for the sake of knowing the procedure. Clearly, the instructions provided to an individual may be as important as what is to be observed itself.

The advantages of observational learning are not limited to observing the surgical procedure done by others, but are also applicable to the surgeon observing his own procedure from a video recording. It has been acknowledged that the best teacher a surgeon can have are his own video recorded procedures and the knowledge of their outcome. This is a vital factor in the context of cognitive techniques, to be discussed later in this book.

Observational learning can sometimes be problematic as some senior surgeons may have acquired their seniority and status on the basis of good management ability or academic achievements but are not quite as technically proficient. Some of these surgeons are of firm belief that they're technically skilled. Whilst this may not be a problem for their peers who recognise the quality of technical 'skills' for what they are, it most certainly can be a problem for more junior surgeons who equate seniority and career success with technical proficiency.

The talent code

At the start of a career, there may be difficulties in acquiring surgical skills for the novice. However, most aspirants eventually attain competency as they improve with experience. A few may progress faster and continue to improve. Some of these 'fast trackers' are eventually hailed as masters. One may wonder, what is the reason behind the variability between mediocre and master performers?

A simple explanation for an exemplary skill is 'a natural gift'. A surgeon has a natural ability, or has 'gifted hands', it may be said. This implies that the quality of surgical skill is largely determined by inherited abilities. Yes, individual effort in attaining skills is recognised, but it is also strongly believed that innate abilities decide the maximum limit for a person's accomplishments (57). How far does the 'inherited upper limit' view concur with reality?

With the introduction of any day-to-day skill, the initial aim is to achieve a level of reasonable competency. The primary aim is to avoid errors. After some practice, big mistakes become rare, performance is smooth and hard concentration is no longer needed to perform. After a reasonable amount of experience, which is less than 50 hours for most day-to-day skills, an acceptable standard is typically achieved. The individual's skills become programmed and can be implemented effortlessly. Because of the automation, performers lose control over implementation, which makes it hard to modify the skill. When the skill learning reaches the final stage, performance attains a plateau and you do not see any significant improvement afterwards. Thus the argument about the influence of innate capabilities may appear to be consistent with everyday skills. Nevertheless, does it apply to professional skills such as surgery?

The main difference between acquiring ordinary skills and professional skills is obviously the time factor. Whereas expertise in day-to-day skills can be achieved quickly, professional expertise takes years to develop. There is no robust evidence to prove that professional achievements are limited by innate ability (58). Neither is there evidence to show that natural abilities that are vital for achieving expertise do not change with deliberate efforts (59). Thus, the belief that genetically determined limits constrain achievable performance has been rejected. On the contrary, studies show that motivated individuals can improve their level of performance far more significantly than what is conventionally presumed.

When factors other than 'natural ability' are considered in surgical settings, another explanation is the number of procedures performed by a surgeon. Most will agree, the greater the number of procedures performed, the better will be the skill. Studies have shown that variability in outcomes is related to the volume of procedures for an individual surgeon (60). However, not everybody is willing to accept these observations at face value. The conclusion that high volume is the cause of the superior performance has been challenged (61). Rather than it being a cause, higher surgical volume is the effect of the superior skills those surgeons possess, it is argued. Accordingly, "less skilled surgeons have more initial failures, which in turn reduce their future opportunities to perform more procedures". Simply put, surgeons with better skills get more cases. "Even among surgeons with high and very high volumes of specific procedures, there are significant individual differences in outcome, far exceeding the variability that would be expected by chance alone" (62). You need experience to become an expert; however, experience does not invariably lead surgeons to become experts. Most professionals improve their performance up to the level of competency. Nonetheless after that stage, improvement appears to be unpredictable and even the volume of experience is not a good predictor of achieved performance.

Continued improvement in achievement is not an automatic consequence of experience. Rather it is the result of aspiring experts seeking out particular kinds of experience, what Ericson called "deliberate practice" (63). The specific aspects of a successful practice involve repetitive performance of a single task, rather than general training in a changing variety of tasks. It's only focused repetitive practice that results in high level performance. Yet that is precisely what surgical training has not been able to provide so far. (3). Deliberate practice involves activities designed with the only purpose of refining particular features of performance. The total volume of deliberate practice is intently associated with the achieved level of performance in various fields. There is no reason that the same would not apply for surgeons.

Taking the quality of performance to an expert level needs the performer to be involved in deliberate practice. Deliberate practice is also necessary to maintain the quality of performance. For consistent improvement in any performance, three conditions need to be fulfilled. First, the performer needs to have motivation and the necessary information to improve. Secondly, feedback on the performance is needed. And finally, one needs opportunities to improve by performing the similar tasks recurrently. Attempts to raise performance past its present state consist of exploring superior techniques to perform.

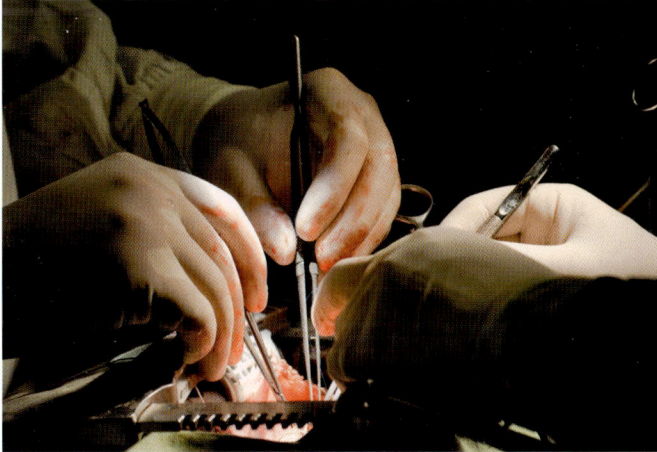

How is it that some professionals reach a performance plateau or remain run-of-the-mill performers, whereas others keep improving their performance? The answer lies in the fact that as individual behaviour becomes automated, conscious control to make intentional adjustments is lost by mediocres, yet experts continue to progress with further practice, together with deliberate practice. The important point for aspiring experts is to prevent the restricted progress accompanying the automaticity and to obtain cognitive skills that will ensue upgrading. The experts neutralise predispositions for automaticity by developing and cultivating cognitive means. The experts consciously pursue conditions in which the objective is to surpass their existing level of performance. They seek means that increase their capacity to oversee their own performance. For example, expert typists look further ahead in the text and are thus able to prepare future keystrokes ahead of time to increase their typing speed. The rapid reactions of expert athletes are not just due to greater speed of their nerve signals, but depend rather on their ability to better anticipate future situations and events by reactions to advanced cues

(64). The same applies to master surgeons who seek challenges of difficult cases or attempt to improve operative results.

As with expertise in other fields, surgical expertise is greatly esteemed since it takes years of hard work to achieve. In music or sports, ten years or ten thousand hours of goal-oriented practice is the minimum requirement - and surgery is not too far in this regard (65). Given the pathway to becoming a master is long, discovering ways to accelerate the speed of gaining of expertise is helpful. Finding more effective methods of teaching surgical skills is effectively a pursuit for ways to fast-track the evolution from non-expert to expert surgeon. Extrapolating the evidence from the research among expert and non-expert surgeons, and from findings of expertise in other areas, Bruce Abernathy (66) has outlined the aspects of surgical skill that differentiate between the two, i.e. expert and non-expert surgeons.

According to Abernathy, an expert surgeon's above average performance is due to cognitive, motor, perceptual and feedback monitoring skills as well as deliberate practice. He recommends that these aspects should be the focal point of surgical skill training, and in deciding how best to provide practice to surgeons to speed up their advancement alongside the path to proficiency.

Cognitive

Studies of experts show many differences from cognitive aspects. Characteristically experts perceive the issues at depth, and devote a significant period in analysing the issues prior coming to conclusion. They show greater awareness of pertinent details (declarative knowledge) and measures (procedural knowledge). Research on surgeons has shown that the determining factor that limits the trainees in comparison with experts is not about knowing what to do, i.e. declarative knowledge, but it is rather about how to do it, i.e. procedural knowledge.

Motor

The actions of experts show more stability compared to non-experts. Experts use external forces, like gravitational forces, more efficiently. This means that they use muscular force only when absolutely needed, thereby ensuring an economy of movement (67). Compared to this, beginners apply force incessantly during the entire period of action which quite often may not be necessary. The neuromuscular configurations of experts, as seen in electromyographs, typically shows distinct spurts of muscle activity and a comparative lack of movement in antagonist muscles. This is the effectiveness, which empowers the experienced to show better fatigue endurance and smoothness of actions (68). These features of expert actions as seen when seniors demonstrate better economy of movement (69). Given that fatigue has been identified as a major challenge in the maintenance of surgical performance, the more efficient movements of expert surgeons may help prevent premature fatigue during an operation (70).

Perceptual

Experts seem to have a greater ability to distinguish between diverse perceptual stimuli, for example differentiating between normal and pathological tissue. It is not only that the experts perceive better than non-experts, they also have better capacity for pattern recognition. Visual pursuit or eye movement patterns of experienced surgeons vary from novices. To position the endoscope at the time of surgery, endoscopic surgeons do not gaze at the endoscope as much as inexperienced surgeons do (30).

Thus far, we have examined surgical skills from range of perspectives. These perspectives are not part of usual considerations in a process of improving surgical skills. Do you remember how you learnt to ride a bicycle? Most likely, your parents or other family members guided you, or you may have tried to ride by yourself from the start. How about driving a car? It must have been a more formal affair than learning to ride a bicycle. You may have had driving lessons and had to pass a formal test before being allowed to drive. Now, if you were to become a professional pilot, your training would be a matter of the utmost gravity. It would involve formal assessments, testing and re-testing and so on.

Well, isn't current surgical practice as advanced and complex as flying a plane? If that is the case, why are we learning skills the way we learned to ride a bike or for that matter, drive a car?

It is time we paid attention to the understanding of a surgical skill and human abilities. All the facets of surgical skill mentioned thus far can be addressed by cognitive techniques described in the following chapters.

Key points

■ Surgical skill is a psycho-motor process and the cognitive part needs due recognition.

■ Skill learning goes through three stages cognitive, associative and autonomous.

■ Alternatively, it can be considered to have four phases unconscious incompetency, conscious incompetency, conscious competency, unconscious competency.

■ Strategies like identification, isolation and improvisation helps in the acquisition of skills.

■ Over time the need of perceptual abilities has grown in relation to surgical skills.

■ Deliberate practice is highly effective in developing expertise.

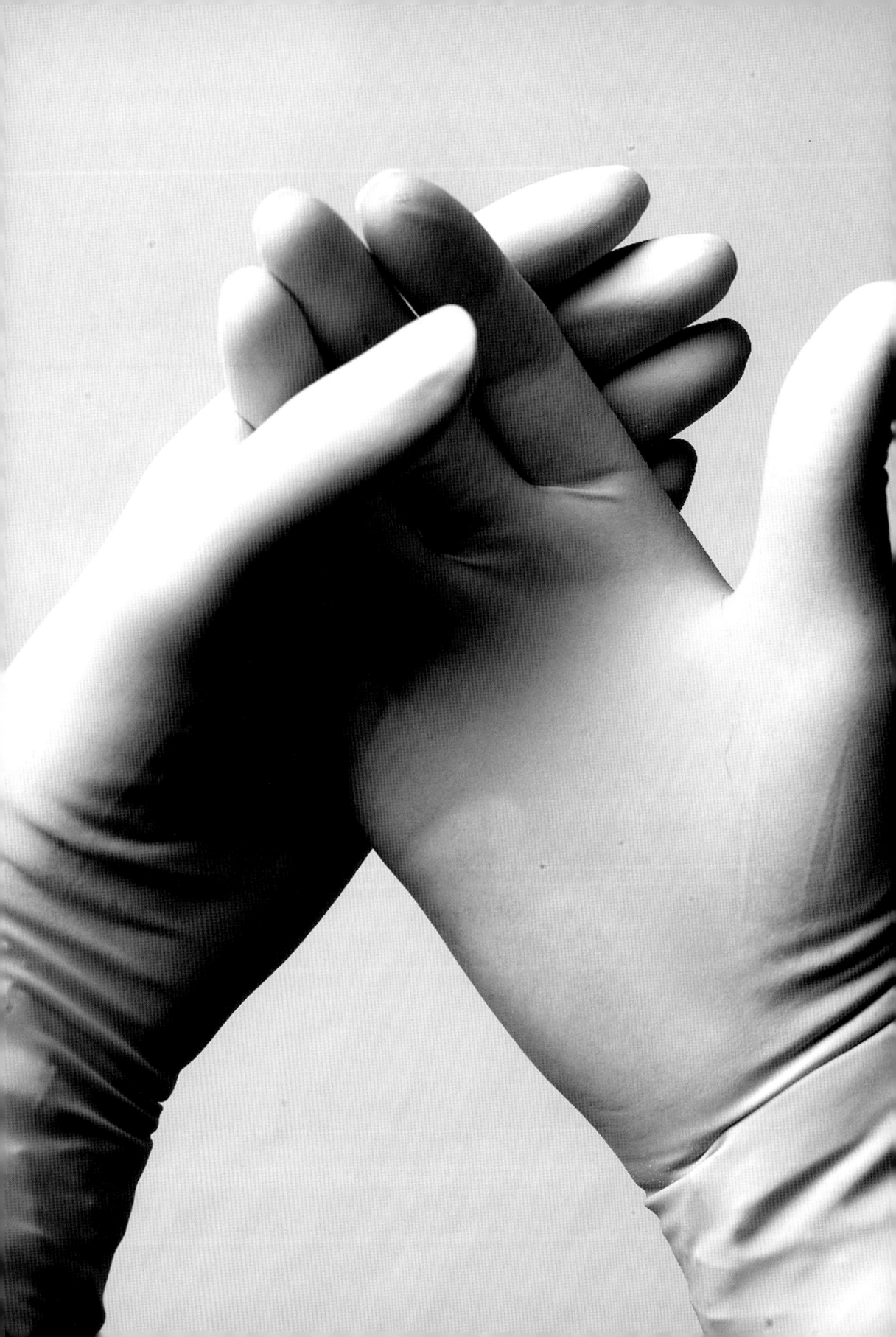

Chapter 3

The mind's eye

How would you answer the following questions?

"Which is the darker green, is it a frozen pea or a pine tree?"
"In which hand does the Statue of liberty hold the torch?"

Please note that you are asked, how the questions would be answered, not what the answers are.

To arrive at answers, you will have to create in your mind the images of peas, a pine tree and the Statue of liberty. Sir Francis Galton, the inventor of fingerprint identification, documented for the first time decades ago, that when asked to recall what was on their breakfast tables, respondents had to visualise the breakfast table to be able to answer. It is almost impossible to recall certain incidents without employing visual thinking. For example, can one answer the following question without using visual thinking?

From which side of the bed did you get out this morning?

Besides recall, visual thinking is used for problem solving as well. To judge if his car can fit into a particular parking space, a driver needs to use visual thinking. In such a situation, an image is 'projected' on to the mental screen just like a slide from a projector.

It is not necessary that the image has to be a still image; it can be a motion picture. If someone is in a shop, thinking about how many curtains would be needed for the house, they would use the visual thinking like a video recorder, going from one window to the next.

Visual thinking is not a passive process. The observer can manipulate the image, if need be. For example, to reply, "Name the letter which is formed when 'N' is rotated clockwise by 90 degrees", you will manipulate the image of 'N' to turn it in to 'Z'.

We rely on visual thinking in everyday life. This reliance is indispensable for a surgeon, for whom its mastery is an essential component of competency. The truth of "surgical thinking starts with the surgeon's eyes," is indisputable. Visual thinking also plays a significant role in the development of surgical intuition and decision-making.

The surgeon skill set in minimally invasive total knee arthroplasty.
The American Journal of Orthopedics, 2006 (71).

Some surgeons rehearse their operations in their 'mind's eye' ahead of time. Surgeons who perform complex surgery go over operation sequences before the surgery – particularly when performing less familiar operations or when learning something new.

Visualisation has been used in sports, music and in other forms of physical performances including dance and even acrobatic flying. Acrobatic pilots not only visualise their flight moves and the controls needed to achieve them, but they also assume corresponding body postures, as if they were experiencing the g-forces and other forces associated with the acrobatic flight manoeuvre.

The correlation between performance of surgeons in visual thinking tests and of surgical skills has been well documented. One study (72) assessed the performance of a group of surgeons on a standardised test of visual thinking and compared it with that of a normative sample. The mean scores for the surgeons were significantly greater than the general population. These results combined with those of previous studies, highlight the importance of high-level visual thinking abilities in surgical competence. In particular, the results show that surgeons exhibit superior proficiency in some specific aspects of visual thinking.

In the following think-aloud excerpt from the book 'Surgical Secrets', a surgeon's response to a clinical situation shows the role of visual thinking in surgical decision-making (73).

Question –

A 30-year-old woman had a laparoscopic cholecystectomy for acute cholecystitis 6 weeks previously. She is now jaundiced with a bilirubin of 14 and an alkaline phosphatase of 350. AST and ALT are normal. What are your thoughts?

Answer –

You would have to be concerned that you have either injured her common duct or left behind a stone in the bile duct. She needs endoscopic retrograde cholangiopancreatography (ERCP) as the next step, which would be diagnostic and potentially therapeutic.

Question –

If an ERCP is not available, what will you do?

Answer -

I would do a transhepatic cholangiogram in an attempt to define where the problem is. Then she will have to have an operation.

Question -
A percutaneous transhepatic cholangiogram shows several clips at the area of the cystic duct stump with a 0.5-cm narrowing of the common duct adjacent to the clips. What do you do?

Answer -
I am trying to visualise what you just told me. You would have to assume a duct injury. I think I would operate on the patient.

Given this description of postoperative complications, the surgeon tried to visualise what had gone wrong. He would have preferred ERCP with its superior visualisation to the static image of the cholangiogram. If it was his own operation, he also might "rewind the video tape", recalling the operation to see if any details of the procedure could explain what was happening now. After receiving a verbal description of the results of the cholangiogram, the surgeon took time to visualise, to create an image of the structures after cholecystectomy. Knowledge from a variety of sources went into this visualisation, including knowledge of the normal anatomy of the organs, the disease that led to the original operation and the typical efficacy of that procedure. It takes time to construct a full visualisation. This was not only because the surgeon was not offered an X-ray, but because it takes time to interpret an X-ray image too. The surgeon did not get a complete picture of exactly what had happened, but could assume it was a duct injury and therefore concluded that an operation was necessary.

Our experiences are symbolised in the brain as images. It is these images that provide insights into how things work, without physically experiencing the actions. Visual thinking is one of the most sophisticated operations conducted by the brain. Forming images is an ability that can be a preparation for an action. Mental images were at the heart of the earliest mental activity, going as far back as the Greek philosophers. Scholars accorded images a special role in thought processes on the basis of introspection, the process

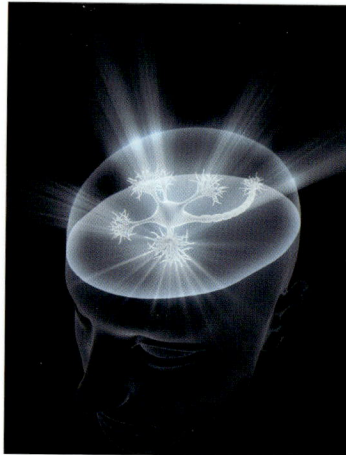

of 'looking within'. The term 'introspection' also highlights the importance of visual thinking in solving problems.

Reliance on visual thinking is so fundamental that it is reflected in expressions such as 'out of sight, out of mind' or 'seeing is believing'. The latter notion is more apt in the context of performance. Someone who sees himself performing well, will believe that he can perform well. However, to believe, do we literally have to see ourselves performing? Well, not necessarily. Seeing in the mind's eye has a similar effect.

Albert Einstein was able to hypothesise the theory of relativity by visualising how the world would look if he travelled inside a beam of light. We know that he did not actually travel at the speed of light. Instead, he was able to perceive the world by imagining he did, which allowed him to believe in his revolutionary theory. Tiger Woods was asked by his father what he was thinking as he was about to play his first shot in his first international tournament. Tiger's answer? "I was thinking about where I wanted the ball to go." He could have been worrying about not hitting the ball correctly, but instead he chose to see himself hitting the ball perfectly. Albert Einstein and Tiger Woods both availed of the advantage of a powerful process - seeing (in the minds' eye) and believing. They harnessed the power of imagination to provide the vision to reach the limits of their potential. For them, "seeing" in the mind's eye was, "believing". It is a technique that programs the body to respond optimally, giving performers the capacity to see and believe, endowing them with the confidence and focus to perform successfully. Most of us possess the ability: but all of us do not use it systematically or effectively enough.

Mental readiness in surgeons and its links to performance excellence in surgery (74).

In this study surgeons from various specialities were interviewed regarding their preparation before surgery. The results showed that some surgeons engaged in visual thinking before an operation but not everybody was able to translate those visual thoughts into what is considered as imagery. Only a few surgeons practiced appropriate imagery. Those surgeons viewed mental imagery as a critical skill that needs to be developed with practice. According to these surgeons, mental readiness played a major role in the success of a surgery. Although various elements are essential for excellence in surgery, there appeared to be an important separator: imagery.

Power of imagination

Imagination is far more powerful than one can imagine! Of course it depends on what kind of imagination is being considered. An imagination could be of two types: active and passive. Passive imagination is just like daydreaming; looking at images floating by without capturing them. In active imagination, on the other hand, one is able to generate detailed images, intentionally. Therefore, it is active imagination that is referred to when we talk about the power of imagination.

A tennis player actively imagines an important upcoming game: he tries to visualise the dark green walls of the court, the smell of freshly mowed grass and even applause from spectators for his winning shots. He is able to conjure up the sensation in his muscles as he plays a powerful shot and sounds of his opponent struggling to reach the volley and his gasps of frustration. In a contrasting scenario, a woman athlete is reminiscing over an accident during a year-old competition. She continues to imagine it happening over and over again despite a strong desire to avoid it. She repeatedly relives the fall from a beam that cost her a medal.

These two contrasting examples prove that imagining a performance has either the power to make chumps out of champions, or raise ordinary performers to their pinnacle. This kind of visualisation can happen spontaneously. Switching it on or off at will may be difficult but not impossible. In one experiment, experienced golfers were divided into three groups. The first group was told to imagine that their shots were dropping into the hole correctly. The second group was briefed to imagine their shots were missing the hole, i.e. a negative outcome. The third group was asked not to imagine anything. The outcome was telling. The golfers who employed positive imagination performed better than those who did not imagine at all. And the golfers who imagined a negative outcome were inferior to the control group (75). It's evident then that an active imagination can be a powerful friend or a dire foe. What is imagined, can make you feel anxious or confident, it can sharpen your focus during performance, motivate you to put in extra efforts or convince you that all is lost. Bringing the power of active imagination under control can enable its use for improvements in performance.

Using imagery to enhance performance is not a new notion, but its acceptance among performers and scientists is relatively recent (76). The first research on imagery dates back to 1931, when experiments showed that imagining bending one's arm would create actual contractions in the flexor muscles. In 1972, Suinn demonstrated that skiers could improve their times with the help of imagery. Subsequent research has shown that imagery can enhance the performance of basketball players, gymnasts, volleyball players, tennis players and golfers. Over the past 30 years, world class athletes from a wide spectrum of sports have confirmed the effectiveness of imagery (77).

Numerous claims about imagery appear to be possible while there are some that are less obviously so. Also, claims that seem possible to some may seem impossible to others. Sorting the wheat from the chaff has proved to be a thorny issue. A major problem in understanding the nature of mental images has been their inherently private nature, which has long prevented objective assessments of their function. This has prompted the dismissal of the notion of mental imagery and its banishment from scientific discussions. It was thought that thinking is no more than a subtle talking to oneself. The inability to consider visual thinking as a thought process meant that these views predominated until new methods offered ways to evaluate thinking. The new technology opened the doors for the objective study of visual thinking. At about the same time, advances in computer science offered new ways to conceptualise human information processing in visual thinking. In the last few years cognitive science has opened up a new stage in the field of imagery. It is mainly Positron Emission Tomography (PET) and Functional Magnetic Resonance Imagery (fMRI) that have opened the doors for an objective testing of imagery.

Imagery in sport

Performance enhancement in sport is synonymous with doping, the use of chemical substances by athletes to enhance their abilities. But do you know that athletes employ imagery more than any other performance enhancement technique? (78) Olympic high jump star Dwight Stones could be seen, eyes closed, head bobbing as he conjured up in his mind the image of his approach and of clearing the bar. The exceptional Alpine ski racer Jean Claude Killy won gold medals in three different Olympics. When injury prevented him from actual practice on the snow, he developed an exceptional ability to prepare for a race with mental practice. In spite of the lack of physical practice, Killy went on to put in one of his best performances. Tennis champion Chris Lloyd who was known for her consistency, used to rehearse her ground strokes mentally before a match.

Some athletes discovered imagery on the advice of professionals. But a number of renowned athletes evolved such techniques on their own as they sought novel ways to enhance levels of performance.

Just how does imagery work for athletes? The legendary golfer Jack Nicklaus said that hitting the ball to a certain place in a certain way was 90 per cent mental. Active imagination is like going to the movies, he'd say. Nicklaus watched a self-produced colour movie in his mind's eye every time he prepared to hit a ball. In his own words, "I never hit a shot, not even in practice without having a very sharp, in-focus picture of it in my head. First I "see" the ball where I want it to finish, nice and white and sitting up high on the bright green grass. Then the scene quickly changes and I "see" the ball going there: its path, trajectory and shape, even its behaviour on landing. Then there is sort of a fade out and the next scene shows me making the kind of swing that will turn the images into reality." (79)

Jack Nicklaus won more major golf championships than anyone else because of his amazing physical talent. But it was his concentration skill that placed him at such an exalted level. Nicklaus' systematic practice of imagery facilitated the concentration that was the key to his success.

World cup ski champion Steve Podborski describes how elite skiers use imagery and why it is such a valuable technique. "Another thing that gets you to the point where you are one of the elite, is the ability to visualise not only the way it looks when you are going down, but how it feels... the muscle tension that you actually go through when you make the turns, and to experience what attitude your body is in... I feel what things will feel like and see everything run through my head. I have a moving picture with feelings and sensations. When I am doing these mental runs... if I make a mistake, I will stop the picture and back it up. Then I run through it and usually get it right the second time. I run through the entire course like that (80).

In competitive athletics winning or losing is a matter of just fractions of a second, where microscopic advantages or disadvantages determine the outcome. Given the huge investments in terms of time and energy and the magnitude of the consequences of winning, i.e. large sums of prize money, the glory and adulation, it is no surprise that athletes today are so desperate in the search for a winning edge in performance. At the elite level, physical abilities are often almost even and then it is the psychological edge that swings things in the winner's favour. Mark Spitz, who won a record seven gold medals at the Montréal Olympics, says, "At this level of skill, the difference between winning and losing is 90 per cent psychological."

Now sports scientists are paying heed to the imagery phenomenon and how it works (81). They have delved into the kinds of imagery athletes use (82), to attain what goals, and the personal and situational factors that facilitate or obstruct the process (83). They sought answers if imagery enhance or hinder performance and how effective it is (84). The evidence affirms that imagery does enhance the learning and performance of a skill as well as competition-related thinking. Imagery helps athletes in routine situations as well as their responses in critical situations. By combining the information from research on athletes' experiences with imagery, scientists have tabulated principles to use imagery effectively besides developing imagery programs.

However, athletes' reactions to using imagery vary from complete trust in its usefulness to out-and-out rejection that it holds any potential whatsoever. Some questions regarding imagery applications have been answered by scientific research, but others necessitate more analysis. Experimental and anecdotal evidence both noticeably show that imagery practice can be a treasured technique in cultivating performance but caution that it must be applied with care as inappropriate use can lead to deleterious effects.

What exactly is it - imagery or mental practice?

At this stage, it will help to be clear about the terminology. Words like visualisation, mental practice, imagery and cognitive simulation are all bandied about, but which is the most appropriate?

Mental practice or Imagery

Mental practice or mental rehearsal initially signified a method other than physical practice. Mental practice involves the repetition of a task without any visible movement. It is a non-specific category of any form of concealed practice. Even "thinking through an action" or "talking one's self through the steps" are considered to be mental practice. To coin a phrase, mental practice is to imagery what still photography is to moving pictures. In contrast to the mental practice method, "close your eyes and think about making the incision", imagery techniques actually seek a full dimensional re-experiencing of the event: "be there in the situation again… so that you are aware of where you are, what is around you, who is with you… you are in the operation theatre, a patient is lying on the table, the anaesthetist is at the head end of the table…" Mental practice could involve non-image based strategies such as verbal rehearsal which may not involve visual imagery at all. Although as a term, 'mental practice' has been employed interchangeably with imagery, let us not forget that imagery is different and qualitatively superior to mental practice.

Could imagery be compared to a dream? Imagery, like a dream, is an experience that can be so real that it is hard to believe afterwards that it was not. Imagery however is different from dreams with regard to the sense of control. A dreamer has no control over his dreams. But the person who decides to use imagery has the sequence of activities under his control. It is as if a person were able to select a specific portion of a movie in which he was filmed, switch on the projector, be instantly transported into the movie, so as to re-experience the entire scene, and yet retain the control of a director who could alter the script.

During imagery an individual is conscious of the experience, as he purposefully generates an image. Daydreaming which we all are prone to do from time to time, occurs in a fully conscious state, but we do not have complete control over the things that we see. It is a temporary detachment from a person's existing situations during which the person's touch with reality is distorted and somewhat replaced by visual fantasy.

Imagery or cognitive simulation can be defined as using all the senses to create or recreate an experience in the mind. This definition contains three keys to understanding imagery.

1. We create as well as recreate experiences in our minds. Thus, imagery is based on memory and we experience it by reconstructing events.

2. Absence of external stimuli - it is a sensory experience that occurs without any environmental props.

3. It is a multi-sensory experience.

Although the term 'imagery' is popular, it does have some limitations. The first is that the word imagery inadvertently emphasizes visual modality more than any other sensory modality. This to some extent defeats the purpose of the process, since it is vital for the process to be multi-sensory. The other problem appears to be the term 'imagery' being indiscriminately used for various unscientific applications. People who look at the imagery with suspicion and consider it to be esoteric cannot be entirely blamed due to the unscrupulous application of the term 'imagery' by some. For these reasons cognitive simulation appears to be the most appropriate term. The word 'cognitive simulation' reflects the scientific nature of the underlying process. It is more suitable in a surgical context considering the use of simulators in surgery. However, in view of its use in the existing literature, its familiarity and convenience, the terms imagery, mental practice and cognitive simulation are used interchangeably in this book. It is expected that after this introduction, the term 'cognitive simulation' will be preferred in the surgical context in future.

Below is the transcript of a surgeon thinking aloud in the presence of surgical trainees (73). It tells how the surgeon uses his hands to visualise the operation, his gestures communicating his visualisation of the operation. This surgeon was thinking with his hands, using them to explain the steps of the operation, indicating where the anatomic features were as he imagined creating spaces and moving organs, showing the position his hands would take as he did those manoeuvres. His description of the operation shows that he remembered it through visual, tactile, and kinaesthetic modalities.

A 65-year-old man has a biopsy-proved adenocarcinoma of the rectum. Tell us how you would do the colo-anal anastomosis.

You open the abdomen. Then the next step is to look at the liver and feel the liver - feel it carefully because 80% of liver metastases are on the surface. The second step is to pick up the omentum, hold it up, and run your fingers down the aorta on either side. You just go "psssp," and if you feel little bumps, you consider the possibility of periaortic nodal spread. The next step is to stick your hand down in the pelvis, behind the bladder. Don't mobilise anything. Just take your hand and push down. Try to feel the tumour. At this point, I take down the splenic flexure. After taking down the splenic flexure, you divide the sigmoid colon at about the junction of the transverse and descending colon. The way to figure out where to divide the sigmoid colon is to pull it up and look for a line heading directly downward between the mesenteric fold and the mesentery. This line is the superior hemorrhoidal fold and the sigmoid artery. You follow it downward until you reach the left colic artery. Then you take the colon and start over - you literally start over. Take out your retractor. Push the colon up at the small bowel, and start over. The next step is to find the ureters at the pelvic rim and to follow them down into the bladder. To do that, you have to cut the mesentery laterally on both sides. Then you pull up the bladder and find a plane between the seminal vesicles, which you usually can't see. But if you get the correct exposure, you can see a fusion plane right there. Take your scissors and cut across it a little bit. And after you open the perineal fascia, take your hand, turn it around, and start pushing the bladder upward while you pull the rectum superiorly. Push up the bladder, and head toward the pubis, pushing it up. If you've done this correctly, you can get in a plane directly on the seminal vesicle in the male. Then you continue downward and find the prostate. Once you are past the prostate, you're gone far enough anteriorly from above. You hold the cut sigmoid colon taut as you can, you go about 5 mm past the sacral promontory, and you make a cut in the mesentery. You open the mesentery a little closer to the rectum on that plane than you thought necessary. Then you start pushing the rectum forward with your hand - first with two, then three, then four fingers. Keep pushing it forward. You go down until you are past the coccyx. At that point you are in the perineum. Now you should be straight up anteriorly into the perineum and straight up posteriorly into the perineum. Next you pull the rectum laterally, with your fingers on either side of the broad ligament. Both the broad ligament, which is between your fingers, and the rectum, which is held opposite, is free and the ureter is lateral. Then you come down at a right angle, taking everything lateral below the ureter. And if you pull properly with your fingers, you'll see the middle hemorrhoidal vessels at the point where they come off the pelvic sidewall. You take them there with clamps. Next the tumour is freed, and you continue downward in that plane until you see levators. You need to be 4-5 cm past the tumour. At that point, everything is freed, and you do a colo-anal anastomosis.

Some surgeons may find it difficult to follow this sort of teaching, because they are unable to think easily with visual imagery. Although some with poor imagery ability may figure out during undergraduate period that surgery will be particularly difficult for them, some of them do end up in surgery. For certain, they will find it difficult to develop the visual sense to the required level.

Below is another think-aloud transcript that reveals the impact of the differences in visual thinking between an experienced and an inexperienced surgeon (73). Two surgical trainees and a consultant surgeon were asked to respond to a clinical scenario. While thinking about the case, the experienced surgeon uses his knowledge of anatomy more than the trainee. Visual thinking too played a more central role in the consultant's use of information. In trying to understand the source of the patient's symptom, the experienced surgeon frequently tries to visualise what is going on internally. Knowledge about the location of previous operations contributed to the surgeon's mental representation of the patient's abdomen.

Please note that this think-aloud has been recorded a few years ago when the use of CT scans was not very common

Question:

A 45-year-old woman presents with abdominal pain and vomiting. The pain awoke her at 4:00 a.m. and has persisted throughout the day. You see her at 4:00 p.m. in the emergency room. She had a hysterectomy 5 years ago and is otherwise healthy. Basic laboratory tests are normal. An X-ray of the abdomen has been reported as 'small bowel obstruction'. What else do you want to ask the patient? How do you want to manage her?

Answers:

Junior surgical trainee (CT) - Her abdominal pain began at 4:00 in the morning. Has she been sick? Does she have fever? When was her last bowel movement? Is she passing gas? I would put in a nasogastric tube to see what kind of output I have from that. Depending on the results I receive from all those things, I would reassess her for further management.

Senior surgical trainee (SpR) - I would try to get more history from the patient: whether this is the first occurrence of this type of abdominal pain, where the pain is located, and the characteristic nature of the pain. I would ask her about the nature of her vomiting. I would find out when her last bowel movement was and whether she has been passing any flatus. I would ask about other symptoms. Does she have dysuria, diarrheoa, or any other recent medical problems, such as the flu, cough, or fever? I would ask about details of her previous hysterectomy. Did they make an incision in her abdomen? Did it go up and down or across? Did they do anything else when they took out her uterus, such as remove her appendix?

Consultant Surgeon - I want to know if the patient has had any episodes like this before. I want to examine her for any external evidence of inguinal hernias, femoral hernias, or obturator hernias. Has she lost any weight? I would include a pelvic exam. I suppose I would ask her if she has any idea about what caused the symptoms. Did she experience any trauma? I would ask other historical questions about abdominal pain. Did they take out her appendix when she had the hysterectomy? Are her ovaries still intact? Is the pain colicky in nature? That will do for starters.

Question:

When you review the X-ray yourself, you notice gas in the colon. The patient tells you she has been passing gas intermittently. What do you do?

Answers:

Junior surgical trainee - It is a partial obstruction. In that case, I would admit her for IV hydration and bowel rest to prevent it from progressing to a complete obstruction. I would obtain a small bowel follow through.

Senior surgical trainee - At this point the abdominal exam would be important to see if she had any localized tenderness or peritoneal signs. I would look at the film carefully to see if she had any evidence of free air in the abdomen, which would suggest perforated viscus. I would make sure she did not have any air in her biliary tree on the film. The abdominal exam would direct me at this point.

Consultant Surgeon - Gas in the colon to me does not necessarily mean that she does not have a small bowel obstruction because the gas could have been there before the obstruction or she could have a little bit of gas going through into her colon. I do not worry about that too much in making the diagnosis. I would probably insert an NG tube. If she was not toxic or septic, with no elevated white count and no fever, I would re-examine her and see what happens.

Question:

You insert a nasogastric tube and watch her overnight. The following morning, the patient is no better, but she has less pain. The NG tube has produced 1200 cc overnight. At this stage, what clinical parameters would help you to decide whether to operate? What would make you operate? What would make you not operate?

Answers:

Junior surgical trainee - Though she feels better, her abdomen is tender and there is a significant output from the nasogastric tube. I would go mostly on the physical examination.

Senior surgical trainee - The four classic factors that we look for in patients with small bowel obstruction are fever, tachycardia, leukocytosis, and abdominal tenderness. If she had any of those signs and has failed a period of conservative management, I would operate. The other alternative is to give her contrast through the NG tube into the small bowel follow through to see if she indeed has a complete obstruction.

Consultant Surgeon - I would repeat the abdominal X-ray, focusing specifically on what had happened to the size of the small bowel. If the small bowel was moderately to largely dilated and had either stayed that way or become larger, I would operate. If the size of the small bowel had become smaller with fewer loops and it looked like the problem may be resolving, I may try another day or two of NG suction. But fundamentally, I would go on the basis of the X-ray of the abdomen.

After listening to the patient's condition the following morning, the consultant surgeon's thoughts about an operation revealed additional differences in his use of visual information. The junior trainee said that she would go mainly on the basis of the examination. The senior trainee was more specific, citing four signs that would prove small bowel obstruction and require operation. The consultant said that a repeat X-ray of the abdomen would drive his decision. The trainees were primarily concerned about the possibility that the bowel may be dead, whereas the consultant was focused on whether the obstruction looks like it will resolve, dead or not. Perhaps because of this different focus, or, more importantly, because of his greater use of visualisation, the consultant was much more explicit about the use of the X-ray information; he would look at the change in the size of the bowel. This proves that experienced surgeons rely on visual information more than inexperienced surgeons do (85).

Up to now, we have sought some understanding about surgical skills and the importance of visual skills in surgical performance. Now the question may be about what can be done to improve visuo-spatial skills. Before we consider the practical aspect, it will be most appropriate to gauge this subject in depth. Cognitive simulation being a subjective matter, a deep understanding will lead to better utilisation. The following chapter contains broad theoretical information about how cognitive simulation works.

Key points

■ Visual thinking is used in surgery in various forms.

■ Deliberate, goal directed imagination has been shown to be very effective in improving performance.

■ Imagery has been scientifically evaluated and has been effectively used by elite athletes.

■ Cognitive simulation has a great potential in improving surgical performance.

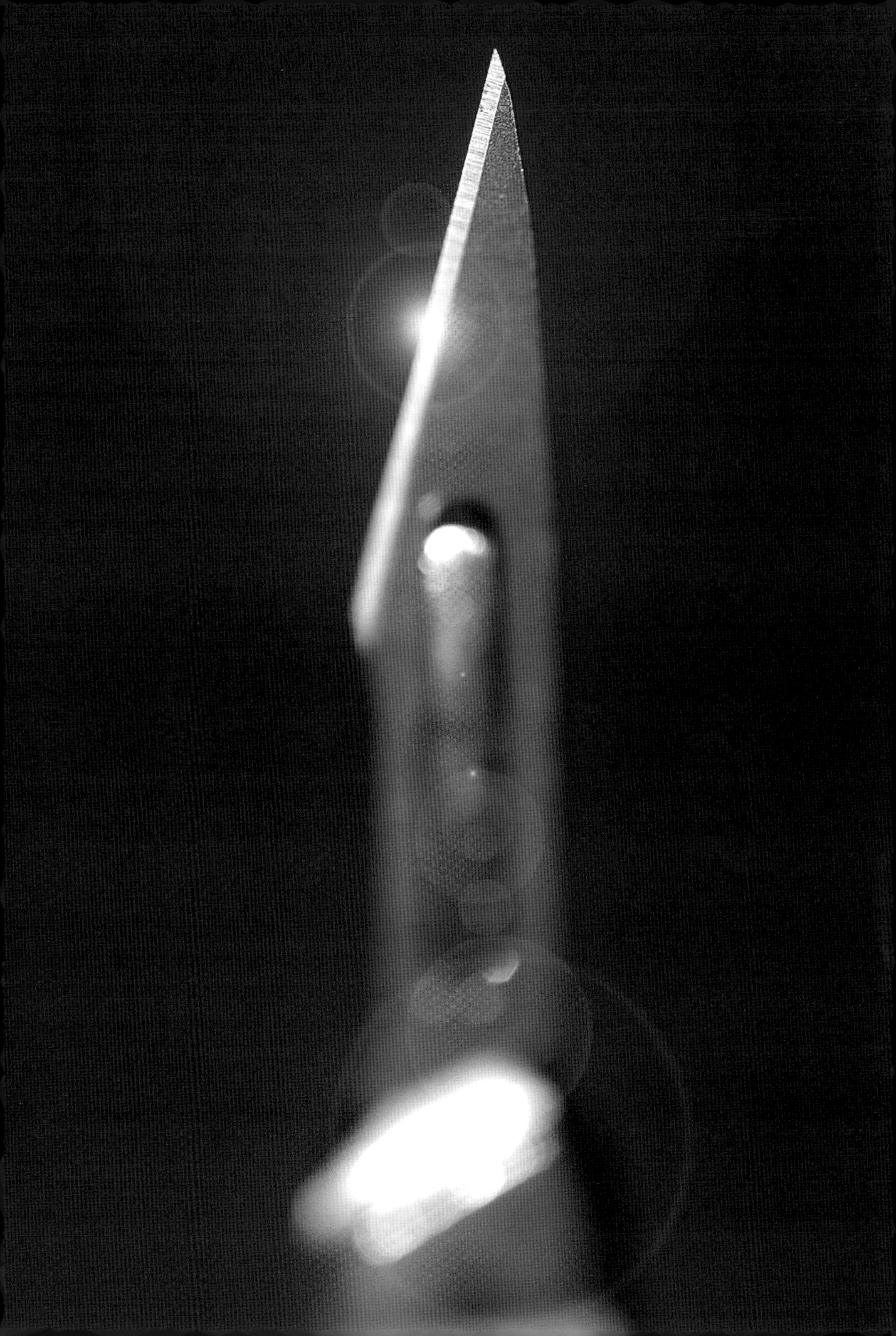

Chapter 4

Theory and research

There is a great deal of evidence to recommend the use of imagery as a means for performance enhancement. But the most important question is, how does it work? How can a sensory experience in the mind enhance the ability to perform? How does seeing and believing enable us to physically carry out these actions? Studies in diverse fields have thrown up explanations of how cognitive simulation facilitates performance. Let us look at how these relate to surgical performance.

Understanding how imagery works will not only remove any doubts, but will also enable its effective application. Understanding the role of the imagination in the successful performance of a task is necessary. Does imagination help in planning movements beforehand, in turn boosting confidence, or does it help by strengthening the motor patterns? Does imagining a performance activate specific neural pathways, resulting in some form of motor preparation? Let us explore the answers to all these questions.

Cognitive science has put forth four main explanations or theories, as follows:

A. Neurological
B. Neurophysiological
C. Cognitive
D. Psychological

A. Neurological explanation

There are three explanations from a neurological perspective.
1. Neuro-muscular theory
2. Symbolic learning theory
3. Bio-informational theory

1. Neuro-muscular theory

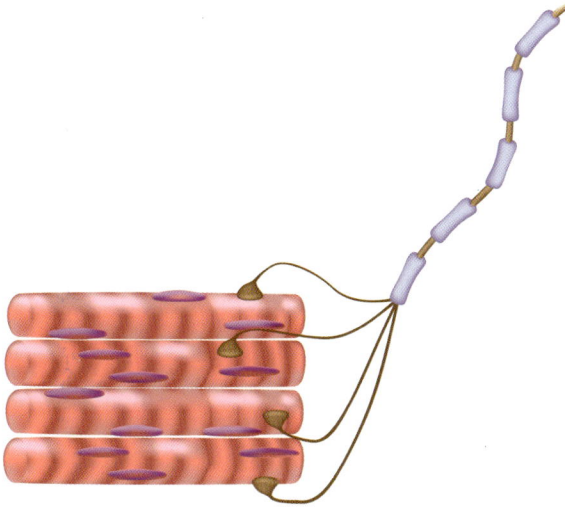

The brain constantly transmits impulses to the muscles during the execution of a movement. The neuro-muscular theory suggests that similar impulses occur between the brain and muscles when one imagines movements without actually performing them. This process is described as 'developing a muscle memory'. Thus, whether the performer actually moves or vividly imagines moving, similar neural pathways are used, although the degree of muscle activity is far less during imagery compared to the actual movement.

Washburn, who proposed this hypothesis (86) argued that the muscle movements resulting from imagining an activity are identical to the movements of an actual activity. Jacobson verified this hypothesis as he monitored muscle activity with the insertion of electrodes in the muscles. When subjects imagined the contraction of an arm, that muscle showed an increase in action potential. Jacobson's research was later supported by Hale (87) and taken forward by Suinn (88), who attached EMG electrodes to a skier's legs, who was then told to imagine skiing along a track. The recorded muscle patterns were strikingly similar to the muscle patterns of a skier who actually skied the course! What is more, by the time the mental rehearsal of the downhill race was completed, the EMG recordings almost mirrored the course itself.

2. Symbolic learning theory

Any movement must first be encoded in the nervous system. There must be a neural plan or mental blueprint for the movement. The symbolic learning proposition suggests that imagery facilitates performance by helping the blueprinting or coding of movements into symbolic components, thereby making the movement more familiar and automatic. In other words, imagery functions as a coding system to help acquire movement patterns.

Sackett who first proposed the symbolic learning theory in 1934, stated that imagery enables performers to rehearse the sequence of movements as symbolic components of a task (89). This has been endorsed by studies which showed greater performance improvement through imagery in tasks that required cognitive processing, as opposed to pure motor tasks. Others like Kohl (90) showed that bilateral transfer of learning occurred after imagery. Bilateral transfer is what occurs when skill practice with one limb enhances the functioning of the opposite limb as well. To illustrate, imagery may be used to practise a skill, such as throwing a ball with the right arm only, but skill improvement is seen in the left arm as well.

The symbolic learning proposition leaves some questions unanswered however. It is easy to see how the encoding of movement patterns through imagery enhances acquisition in the earlier stage, but it does not explain how performance is enhanced by imagery in experienced performers, who already have the movement pattern well established. The other point being, it is impossible to classify movements as strictly cognitive or strictly motor, since most of the movements are on the cognitive-motor continuum.

Is imagery more beneficial to novices or experts?

The early stages of skill learning are primarily cognitive. Thus if the benefits of imagery are primarily cognitive, imagery is expected to benefit more in the early stages. However, an opposing view states that experienced performers find imagery more effective, because they have a more accurate image of the performance.

Feltz and Landers in their meta-analysis (91) calculated the effectiveness of imagery based on a participant's experience with the task, and discovered no significant differences between more experienced and novice participants, when averaged across tasks varying in cognitive elements. They found a slightly larger effect size for more experienced participants, although that of novices was also significant. The authors concluded that the effects of mental practice occur in both early and later stages of learning.

In another meta-analysis, Copper found no significant difference between the performers. Their data showed moderate effect for both novice and experienced participants (92).

3. Bio-informational theory

Lange's bio-informational theory employs an information-processing model. It proposes that an image contains a stimulus scene as well as a response scene. The stimulus scene contains information about the situation or the circumstances before the action takes place. The response scene holds the response or action in that situation. Let us suppose the stimulus image to be a bleeding vessel and the response image to be ligation of the blood vessel. Thus, the brain has a template of stimulus and response for any action to be performed. By engaging in imagery, a stimulus programme is activated that describes the content of the image, and then a response programme that describes what the responses are to the stimuli in that situation. For example, a surgeon imagines that all the necessary preparation for him to start the procedure is complete (stimulus scene) after which he imagines making an incision (response scene).

For cognitive simulation to facilitate a performance, the response programme must be activated so that it can be strengthened. By repeatedly accessing response programmes for a particular stimulus situation and modifying these responses to represent the perfect execution of a skill, imagery helps to enhance the performance. The term 'response set' could be used in the context of this theory. Practically speaking, imagery can be considered as a way of enhancing performance by programming responses to specific situations or creating the perfect response set.

The bio-informational theory is bolstered by the finding that experienced performers benefit more from imagery than novices (91). Experienced performers are expected to have well established behaviour prototype of movements. Imagery improves performance by accessing the prototype information and activating the correct response. Less experienced performers have a vague behaviour prototype that is bound to affect the desired performance adversely.

B. Neurophysiological explanation

During the application of imagery, there is an awareness of bodily sensations and there is an awareness that you are the one who is creating these sensations. Beyond this conscious awareness, changes in biological parameters occur at an unconscious level. Such unconscious alterations are prominently seen in the autonomic nervous system that can only be detected by neurophysiological tests. Thanks to sophisticated neurophysiological tests such as positron emission tomography (PET) and regional cerebral blood flow scans, there is now a greater understanding of the relationship between imagery and movement. The results of the neurophysiological tests revealed that imagery and actual movement are very similar, to the extent that they can be considered as functionally equivalent (93). In other words, it could be said that imagery enhances performance because imagery and physical performance are identical, with the only difference being that in imagery, there is no execution. All in all, the imagery process is akin to physical practice except for the final execution of the motor commands generated by the brain.

PET scans during imagery

From a neurophysiological view, there is no difference between monitoring the function of an organ during imagery or during a physical action. The two types of functional equivalences commonly referred to are visual and motor. There is valid evidence of the functional equivalence of visual imagery and visual perception (94). Similar activations of the occipital regions have been recorded during the performance of visual perception and visual imagery tasks (95). Motor images have the similar functional correlation to the imagined action. It can be said that the benefits of motor imagery on motor execution are due to refining the synaptic efficiency. This results in an increased capacity to tune motor neuronal activity and sharpen co-ordination between agonist and antagonist muscles. Accordingly, the peripheral EMG activity during imagery is more of a result rather than a reason of the learning process.

Because of the same neurophysiological substrate, acquiring skill by performing is not dissimilar from acquiring it through imagery. The evidence for this is documented in studies that utilised central measures of neurophysiological activity, discovering that cortical activation during motor imagery occurs in areas related to motor control and that the activity follows a specific pattern that closely resembles the execution of action (96). The strongest evidence for the functional equivalence of motor imagery and motor preparation probably exists in understanding the role of the supplemental motor cortex in motor imagery. As it is involved in the assembling an established motor pattern, the activation of the supplemental motor cortex highlights the equivalence (97).

Neurophysiological tests not only provide insights into the imagery process, but also unveil the factors associated with the variability of individual imagery abilities.

Eye movements

If imagery is part of the perceptual process, it should include eye movements. Experiments have proven that eye movements during imagery are not just the by-product of the imagery process, but that they actively contribute to the process of image generation. Experiments have shown that eye movements scanned during imagery, correlate to those of actual perception. Rodionov (98) recorded eye movements during a mental rotation test and showed that they serve as an objective sign of individual performance, to be considered as an objective assessment of the quality of imagery.

Autonomic Nervous System and imagery

Movements are planned before they are executed. It is the Autonomic Nervous System (ANS) that provides the momentum to make the execution possible according to the plan. The electro-dermal activity of shooters, as they prepare to fire, show that its level varies as a function of 'being charged' before the shot was fired (99). The best performers' pre-shot electro-dermal levels were lower than those who performed poorly. Thus, imagery can be considered as the first phase of a movement, since preparing for the execution includes a mental rehearsal of the planned movement. Imagery that occurs before the movement, mobilises the ANS into action as if the movement is being performed.

Another study discovered that top shooters' pre-firing concentration phase elicited autonomic responses very similar close to those during the actual shot-making (100). This almost identical nature of ANS responses during the concentration and actual shooting is evidence of the fact that these marksmen could recall memorised routines of shooting by imagining the forthcoming motor sequence, to exert greater control over the execution stages. What's more, they performed more accurately when the autonomic response during the concentration period matched the one during the actual shooting.

The analysis of these elite shooters' autonomic responses lends credence to the idea that the imagery process during the preparation phase sets in motion changes conforming to variations in arousal. This is also true with a simple activity like walking. Recordings of cardiac and respiratory activity show a proportionate increase with the mental effort of the imagery experience. The outcomes of numerous experiments prove that motor imagery performance correlates with variations of autonomic indicators.

Electroencephalogram

With functional MRI it is possible to identify the brain regions activated during imagery. The ability to identify the involved brain structure with high spatial resolution is the biggest benefit of functional MRI. However, given the poor temporal resolution, it is difficult to address questions concerning functional organisation. Electroencephalogram (EEG) provides a measure of neuronal activity with high temporal resolution. It is therefore used to study the dynamic aspects of movement-related activity of the involved areas. Changes in the brain oscillations allows us to see the time course of neuronal activity, before, during, and after an imagined action. Such studies have consistently corroborated the functional equivalence between execution and imagery. Since EEG in turn has poor spatial resolution, a combination of MRI and EEG is complimentary.

Studies using mental chronometry (science of measuring time) provide a common basis for mental imagery and mental execution. The executed and imagined writing of the same number of words, or executed and imagined walking of identical distances take the same amount of time (101). Fitts' Law, which states that a more complex or lengthier movement takes more time to execute than an easier one, also holds for an imagined movement (102). For example, two persons throwing an imaginary ball at different targets, say 10 metres and 50 metres distance, it is the one imagining the longer distance that will take more time (even for imagination).

C. Cognitive explanations:

1. Dual-coding

According to dual-coding theory (103) thinking comprises of the activity of the verbal code, i.e. language and the activity of a non-verbal code. The non-verbal code involves other senses including the visual. Hence images are effective as a means of learning because they provide two independent memory codes, either of which can result in a recall. Knowledge is likely to be best retained when it is encrypted jointly, as language and images.

Stored in memory, both the word 'ball' and the image of a ball can be retrieved from memory with ease. Likewise it may be possible to learn movement sequences both verbally and through images. There exists evidence that the two memory codes are independent; one could be forgotten while the other is retained (104).

2. Insight theory

A performer must be able to conceptualise the entirety of a procedure to improve a skill. According to the insight theory, imagery helps in focusing on the general impression of the skill in addition to the details of the movement. This explains why previous experience enhances the benefits of mental practice. Improvement in performance is not always in direct proportion to the amount of time devoted to practice. Rather, it's seen that learning comes about with the changes in behaviour over time, which is a result of insight. Insightful behaviour is known to occur after periods of practice. Mental practice will not only ensure learning, but provide for a new perceptual organisation through insight (105).

3. Attentional-arousal explanation

This explanation of how imagery works is not a theory but an intuitive description of the role of imagery in helping performers reduce performance anxiety and improve attention (106). The term 'mental set' can be used in this context, and it can be said that imagery does elevate performance by creating the right mental set. An optimal state of arousal allows the execution of peak performance, and imagery facilitates the setting of arousal at an optimal level. Imagery also enables the focus on the task necessary for optimal performance, by screening out potential distractions.

D. Psychological explanation

Confidence in one's abilities is indispensable for superior performance. Self-confidence reflects the perception of one's overall capability. However, when it's the confidence regarding a specific task, the appropriate term is self-efficacy. A surgeon could be said to be self-confident in performing orthopaedic surgery, but to describe his level of confidence in a shoulder arthroscopic surgery, self-efficacy would be the right term. The correlation between self-efficacy and imagery suggests that imagery increases a performer's expectation of success, that leads to an eventually successful performance. Expectations of success are based on your own successful past performance successes, or observing other's successful performance. Imagining oneself performing a task successfully is similar to observing someone else perform the skill (modelling), which therefore reinforces and boosts expectations of success. Increased self-efficacy is known to enhance performance (107). Studies in range of skills have shown that imagery enhances self-confidence (108).

Finally, delving deep into theoretical understanding should have answered some questions regarding the basis of cognitive simulation. But it is also likely that new questions may arise. Well, there is more evidence to come on the following pages to prove that cognitive simulation works, and that it's not just an illusion in someone's mind'!

Key points

■ Cognitive simulation is a multi-faceted topic with a range of theories that explain the phenomenon.

■ Over the last few years significant progress has been made in the understanding of imagery via scientific processes.

■ Research comprehensively documents the validity of imagery in performance improvement.

Chapter 5

It's not 'all in the mind' - The evidence

There is no disputing the virtues of a sound theoretical base, but providing evidence that an intervention works is altogether different. Since it is not possible to observe cognitive simulation directly, indirect methods must be used. This creates difficulties in the surgical context, as results are likely to be affected by a number of variables. It becomes necessary then to extrapolate evidence from other disciplines, before looking into the evidence from surgery.

Evidence from performance studies

Even a cursory review of the literature shows the basic paradigm of mental practice studies as -

1. Physical practice, when subjects practise the task a fixed number of times
2. Imagery, when subjects mentally rehearse the task the same number of times
3. The control, when subjects receive no physical or imagery practice (109)

In most of the studies, subjects are randomly assigned to one of these categories and subsequently re-tested. In general, the outcomes have been quite consistent across various studies that have used this paradigm. Physical practice has a greater effect on performance than imagery practice, which in turn is better than no practice at all (110). Examining the effect of combining imagery and physical practice, and comparing it to physical or imagery practice alone, is an extension of this paradigm. The combination group alternates between physical and imagery practice, with 50:50 as the standard ratio. An amalgamation of mental practice and physical practice ensures far improved results than mental practice or physical practice only (111). Durand and Hall re-examined the data and argued that it may be possible to replace some physical practice with imagery practice, without affecting the performance enhancement that normally ensues after physical practice (112).

In a study that involved musical instrument training, one group was given actual practice for five days, while the other group was given imagery training along with physical practice. It was seen that the training in both groups resulted in increased cerebral activity of hand muscles (113). The group involved in physical practice showed a vast increase in performance, but the imagery group also showed improvements. In the next phase, perhaps of greater interest, the imagery group was given an additional practice session, and their performance was found to be on par with the active group. This does validate the concept of combining imagery and actual practice as shown in other studies (114).

Evidence from neurology

Cerebral injury patients have been under the medical research scanner for over a century, offering useful data on how the brain uses imagery. Some patients were unable to engage in visual thinking after losing their sight, and parallel deficits in imagery and actual perception were typically observed. Patients with cerebral deficits were unable to discriminate colours, either perceptually or in imagery, while others were unable to recognise faces either perceptually or in imagery. Such studies concluded that "visual imagery and visual perception share many common mechanisms. However, imagery, unlike perception, does not require the low-level organisational processing that occurs in the retina: and perception, unlike imagery, does not require the use of memory when a stimulus is not present." (115)

Neuroimaging studies that have compared imagery and perception, confirm the findings of the studies on patients with cerebral damage. One study found that about two-thirds of all the cerebral cortex area activated during perception as well as in imagery, remained the same (116). However others show that imagery and perception do not always activate the same cerebral areas, and are seen to have some unique regions. Lesions in the cortical regions not activated by both perception and imagery therefore produce deficits when imagery or perception is interrupted separately, while injuries in the regions activated in common generate parallel problems in imagery and perception.

Motor disability is frequently observed in patients who have suffered a stroke. The acquisition of motor control is a key aspect of a stroke patient's rehabilitation. The fact that imagining limb movement can activate primary motor areas opened a new front on the restoration of movement in patients with motor dysfunction. Motor imagery is one of the therapeutic tools used to recover motor impairment after a stroke where recovery occurs by neural reorganisation in the damaged cortex (117). This reorganisation depends on the information delivered by sensorimotor feedback loops. However, the feedback system is not the only way to activate the motor neurons, it can also be activated 'offline' by imagining movements (118). The discovery of mirror neurons, which fire when an individual is observing someone else's movements, confirms that our action system can be used 'online' as well as 'offline'. Thus, imagery works as a 'backdoor' access to the motor system. Indeed, combining the evidence from patients who have suffered from a stroke strengthens the notion that imagery promotes the rehabilitation of a limb function (119).

Pyramidal neurones within the motor cortex form part of the cortico-spinal pathway that transmits descending voluntary drive to motor neurones in the spinal cord. The excitability of the cortico-spinal pathway can be measured with Transcranial Magnetic Stimulation (TMS). TMS activates pyramidal neurones trans-synaptically and elicits a motor-evoked potential (MEP) in the relevant muscle, that can be recorded by electromyography. The amplitude of MEP reflects the excitability of the cortico-spinal path. Cortico-spinal excitability is facilitated during imagery in a way that parallels the facilitation observed during actual performance: specific to the muscles involved in task performance; graded according to their contribution to the movement and occurring within a similar time frame. Together, these observations strongly suggest that the neural mechanisms that modulate cortico-spinal excitability during voluntary movement are also operational during motor imagery.

Some part of studies on the neural basis of imagery is devoted to find out if the early visual cortex is stimulated while performing imagery (120). The early visual cortex encompasses the first two cortical areas that accept inputs from the eyes. A significant number of neuro-imaging studies show that the early visual cortex does get stimulated during imagery (121).

Evidence from surgical studies

Anecdotal reports from surgeons reveal that they use mental practice strategies informally by 'going over' the planned operation in their head prior to the operation itself. Notwithstanding the obvious use of imagery by surgeons, there is little research to prove the efficacy of mental practice in the surgical literature. One of the earliest studies examined the comparative effectiveness of variable amounts of physical practice and mental practice in acquiring surgical skills (122). The aim of this study was to ascertain if physical practice and imagery practice were equally successful in acquiring surgical skills and transferring them to actual surgery. 65 second-year medical students were randomly divided into three groups and they received one of the following:

Three sessions of physical practice on suturing a pig's foot
or
Two sessions of physical practice and one session of mental imagery rehearsal
or
One session of physical practice and two sessions of imagery rehearsal.

After these sessions the subjects operated on a live rabbit. The group which engaged in mental rehearsal after physical practice, performed just as well as those who had additional physical practice. The conclusion therefore was that physical practice followed by imagery practice is a better alternative for training in surgical skills as it eliminates the effort and cost of additional physical practice.

Another study (123) compared imagery rehearsal with the textbook study of a procedure. 64 second-year medical students were divided into two groups in a random manner. One group was assigned to conduct imagery while the other did a textbook study. Both groups were offered the usual skills training including lectures, demonstration, and physical practice on pig's feet. The imagery group was given further training in imagery while the other group was asked to study the textbook. The analysis of variance on the subjects' performance in live surgery showed a significant correlation in favour of the imagery group over the textbook study group.

The results of the first randomised controlled trial of mental practice were published in 2007 in the *Annals of Surgery*. It evaluated if cognitive training had any impact on the performance of simulated surgical procedure (124). A pre-test and post-test design was used to test the effect of mental training for laparoscopic cholecystectomy. Each participant performed the procedure once on a virtual reality trainer before undertaking the baseline procedure. This step helped all the subjects to become familiar with the simulator. After all subjects underwent the baseline procedure, they were allocated in a random fashion to one of the following three groups:

1. Control group - no additional training
2. Practical training group - practical training session on the simulator for 90 minutes and an additional 30 minutes studying written material of the procedure
3. Mental training group - participants from this unit received personalised mental training that lasted for one and half hour with senior surgeons who were trained in mental training by psychologists experienced in this field

The surgical trainers introduced the concept of mental training and the participants were given the operation primer, which contained a detailed description of the procedure. The procedure was divided into specific steps, with some steps assigned as 'nodal points', i.e. vital steps which needed to be executed precisely in a specific order without much freedom of movement. Specific motor directions and detailed recognition of possible risks were then allocated to every nodal point. Then subjects were given 30 minutes to study the primer on their own.

The primer contained instructions for both motor actions and mental training. The mental training involved four different types:

1. External observational learning - the trainee observes an expert performing the procedure
2. Internal observational learning - the trainee visualises himself performing the procedure
3. Verbal imagery - the trainee creates a image of the action with the help of self-talk (see page 135). The subjects remembered the diction in the primer through self-talk
4. Ideomotor training - the participant visualised the action from an internal perspective (see page 137)

The subjects then performed a follow-up procedure on the simulator. Video recording of every procedure was done and was evaluated independently by four surgeons. Objective structured assessment of technical skills (OSATS) was used for evaluating the simulated surgical procedures.

Out of the total of 98 surgeons, 31 were enrolled in mental training, 32 in practical training and 35 were in the control group. All three groups were homogenous in terms of baseline characteristics. A statistical analysis of the results showed that there was significant improvement in performance in the mental training group, but not in the practical training group. (Even the investigators were surprised with this finding!). Mental training accomplished superior results compared to the other groups in the task specific checklist.

The findings of this study are comparable with the results in sport science which have shown that mental imagery is more helpful for cognitive rather than motor tasks - and the greater the cognitive components, the better the result. Which shows that the more mental processing a procedure needed, the more effective the mental training. On the other hand, the more an action calls for strength, the less efficient mental training would be. Surgical procedures are prime examples of tasks with significant cognitive components. This research showed that cognitive simulation results in a greater enhancement in the cognitive aspect of an operation, (revealed in the task specific checklist), compared to the motor element, which was measured by a global rating scale.

The improvement was particularly evident at specific nodal points like inserting the trocar and exploring the liver and incising the peritoneal lining of the infundibulum. These specific steps are critical in this procedure. Thus, it is clear that imagery improves performance at critical steps. Researchers maintain that this benefit could be the result of the greater functional mental representation of the operation offered by cognitive simulation.

The authors concluded that the benefits of mental training are numerous: cognitive rehearsals cost less than practical training, and once a surgeon has the skills, he can use this technique by himself. Moreover, this skill can be simply transferred to another tasks without any cost. The authors recommend that mental and physical teaching need to be merged, as in sport, and that it be considered as a critical part of training.

Recently a pioneering study to develop mental practice (MP) as a training method was undertaken in London, led by Professor Darzi (125). As part of the study, a cognitive 'walkthrough' of the procedure was undertaken to recognise the important visual and kinaesthetic clues for the operation. The information derived from this 'cognitive walkthrough' was used to develop a 'script', which provided the core contents of imagery. As part of the validation of the script, participants were asked to mentally rehearse the procedure for approximately half an hour. The individual's capacity to mentally practise was measured before as well as after the training with a valid questionnaire. Twenty participants took part in the study, including 10 experienced and 10 novice surgeons. When the questionnaire was tested for reliability the results showed internal consistency. Senior surgeons marked greater on all questions than the trainees before and after the training. This finding confirmed the construct validity of the questionnaire. A substantial increase in global score after imagery was displayed by expert and novice surgeons, indicating both face and content validity. It also showed that "novice surgeons improved significantly in their knowledge, confidence and imagery after MP training. Experienced surgeons, although starting from significantly higher initial imagery scores, also improved in their confidence and kinaesthetic feeling for performance of the procedure."

The importance of this study can be appreciated by the fact that previous studies on imagery had encountered methodological problems that this study was able to overcome. It included experienced surgeons besides trainees, just as sport psychologists involve elite athletes. The use of an imagery script was purposefully designed to improve the methodology of the study, and using a questionnaire to assess the participants' perception of their imagery experience helped to overcome methodological limitations. The authors of the study concluded that mental practice is a time- and cost-efficient approach that increases a surgeon's capacity to visualise them performing a procedure, improving their knowledge as well as confidence.

Prof Darzi led another ground breaking randomised controlled study to determine if mental practice actually improves surgical skills (126). The twenty trainees recruited from a London university hospital did not have prior active involvement in performing laparoscopic surgery. The participant's baseline skills were all comparable. They were given basic information about laparoscopic procedures. This training offered them an essential 'declarative' knowledge of the laparoscopic cholecystectomy. Then they had a 'hands on' training on a simulator which offered 'procedural' knowledge. Following this, all participants were assigned randomly to an intervention (MP) arm or a control arm. All participants practiced one procedure every day on a simulator for five days. Prior to each session, participants in the intervention group conducted mental practice for half an hour. Each participant from the control group spent the same amount of time with a faculty member, during which time they were asked to conduct an academic activity. Since all participants were engaged in some kind of activity, they were oblivious to the fact that they were either in the intervention or control group, ensuring blind control. Every subject from the intervention group was trained in MP using a mental practice script. The script depicted steps of the procedure, and also highlighted the related clues intended to improve the mental representation of the skill.

The main outcome of the study was the quality of performance during the five LC procedures. All the procedures were recorded and were sent to experienced surgeons for evaluation adhering to blind protocols. They used the generic Objective Structured Assessment of Technical Skills (OSATS) based global rating scale to. A validated Mental Imagery Questionnaire (MIQ) was used to evaluate the quality of the mental imagery. Items assessed by the imagery questionnaire included:

Mental readiness to perform the procedure;
Confidence
Usefulness of training
Visual imagery and
Kinaesthetic imagery.

As far as the findings are concerned, the baseline skills amongst participants were equal. When the final results were evaluated, a detailed exploration of the learning curves showed that both groups improved to some extent. However, the control group did not improve further after the second session, while the MP group continued to improve even after five sessions. When the quality of performance (OSATS-based global rating score) was compared, it showed that the MP group was considerably better than the control group during all sessions. This suggested a noteworthy positive association amid greater quality of cognitive simulation and the quality of performance.

The outcome of this experiment demonstrated that imagery improves the quality of surgical performance. This study is remarkable for various reasons. First, this is a pioneering work in surgery that has effectively proven that better surgical performance can be achieved by applying a scientifically created imagery script. This script will help those who may be interested to benefit in improving performance with this method. This is an important aspect for trainers to take into account while considering imagery as a training tool. Another important aspect about this study was that the MP group got better in more than just dexterity – it enriched the overall quality of their performance. This signifies that cognitive simulation was a superior learning method. Besides, substantial associations came to light between mental practice and performance results, suggesting that the superior performance seen in the imagery group was because of the superior imagery, which adds a note of reliability to this research.

These findings reflected those implied by other studies but, importantly, overcame previous methodological flaws. The significance of this study was confirmed by the application of a validated MP protocol and the inclusion of an active control group. It is also significant since they checked the quality of manipulation using validated questions. This factor is very important in the case of research about cognitive simulation since this process is difficult to detect openly; results need to be deduced from different methods. This is the first study in surgery that empirically ensured that the MP group did indeed have better imagery and "imaged what they were supposed to image" rather than making assumptions that this was the case.

The evidence we have seen so far from sports science, neurology and surgery should convince anyone who views it with an open mind. After acquiring general information about cognitive simulation and conclusive evidence about its effects, the next endeavour is to seek practical information about using the techniques in practice.

Key points

■ There is a satisfactory evidence in the literature to prove the efficacy of imagery.

■ In view of the commonality of psycho-motor aspects of the skills, research findings from other related fields can be extrapolated to a surgical context.

■ Although the number of studies done in surgery is small, the results are very encouraging.

Chapter 6

Designing a personal simulator

We have seen that similar cerebral structures are involved in cognitive simulation and physical movements. This means that the more imagined experience reflects what happens during a performance, the better imagery will work. Several elements are involved, the most important being the ability to create good quality images and manipulate them. Another vital factor is the ability to focus without interruption and to be able to keep distractions under control.

Cognitive simulation is a multi-faceted topic. It is important to distinguish individual facets, though, once you start applying imagery, many will be combined. This may be like, begining by putting things into separate boxes, only to mix and match the contents in one box later. If you are able to make the information work, it is like having a custom designed personal simulator, for your exclusive use, available any time, it takes up no room and above all, costs nothing!

Before we start looking at the components of this simulator, let us consider the most basic factor, the individual's ability to conduct cognitive simulation.

Imagery ability

With the exception of about 10% to 12% of the population, the rest of the population is capable of creating images. What does vary however is the quality of images (127). Also, some may find the kinaesthetic modality more difficult to get to grips with, than the visual (128). The good news is that imagery abilities can improve with effort. In that sense, to be precise, imagery is a skill and not an ability. So what is the difference? Well, a skill improves with effort, while a natural ability is difficult to transform. In practice however, both these terms are used interchangeably, without dwelling on their specific meaning, and so is the case in this book.

The interaction between experience and genetic variability is what spawns individual differences in imagery. There exists a reciprocal relationship between the use of imagery and ability, i.e. people with better abilities are more likely to use imagery. But it is also a fact that frequent practice will subsequently result in greater imagery ability (129). Knowing how significantly imagery affects the outcome, it is vital to be able to exercise control over the imagination to improve performance.

Measuring imagery ability

Measuring individual ability will be a step in the right direction since the quality of and the variability in imagery ability does affect performance. Individual differences have been gauged by the means of questionnaires wherein participants engage in imagery and rate their experience. The Vividness of Visual Imagery Questionnaire (VVIQ) is extensively used as a valid and reliable measure of individual differences in visual imagery.

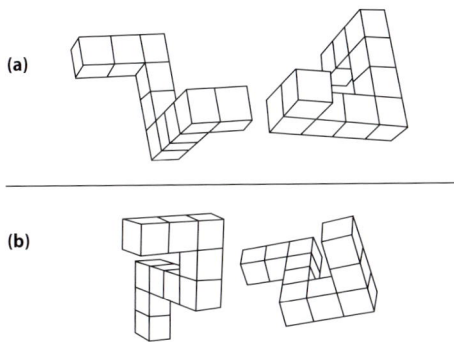

(a)

(b)

Mental Rotation Test - Are these two figures the same except for their orientation?

Another commonly used method of assessing imagery ability involves mental rotation tests where subjects choose options based on imagery. Mental rotation is manipulation and spatial transformation of the imagined object, and subjects are usually asked if pairs of visual 3D stimuli seen from two different angles are identical or not (130).

The application of imagery is known to vary according to individual expertise and ability. There is compelling evidence to prove that experts use imagery far more often than novices do, not to mention that experienced performers tend to have better imagery qualitatively (131). The benefits from imagery for novices meanwhile may be limited owing to the lack of experience in the use of imagery, the skill itself or both. Some observers have detected a positive linear relationship between experience levels and the frequency of imagery use. Others perceive a cyclical relationship between imagery use and ability, i.e., participants with high imagery abilities are more likely to use imagery, while performing imagery will eventually bolster imagery ability (132). The relationship between imagery ability and motor skill performance indicates that better imagers tend to perform better (133).

Is it possible to identify expert imagers objectively?

A study attempted to differentiate experts and non-experts in visual imagery objectively. As a part of this study, participants were asked to learn a map of an island and then were asked to reconstruct a mental image of the map to estimate the distances separating specific landmarks. The results showed that participants who were identified as high imagers from other investigations showed increased patterns of activation in the brain during imagery than low imagers (134). Another study compared the patterns of brain activation during auditory imagery in experienced and novice musicians. Compared to skilled imagers, poor imagers used cerebral processing less efficiently while performing imagery and performance (135).

In view of the significance of imagery ability, an objective ability test would be ideal. However due to the unavailability of such test, scientists have resorted to explore whether subjective test results corroborate with the results of objective investigations. It is known that there are differences in neural activity among better imagers compared to poor imagers. Studies have found that individual differences in VVIQ scores, i.e. a subjective test, can be used to predict changes in a person's brain while visualising different activities. Functional magnetic resonance imaging (fMRI) was used in a research to study the association between visual cortex activities while participants conducted imagery. Reported image vividness correlated with the fMRI signal in the visual cortex. Thus it confirmed that individual differences in the VVIQ could be measured objectively (136) and that the subjective tests are valid. Overall these results support the existence of distinct neural mechanisms of expertise in imagery, as a function of the individual skill level and justify the use of subjective tests to assess the ability.

Dimensions of cognitive simulation

A skilled surgeon accurately processes volumes of sensory data during a performance that guides his actions and regulates movements. The art of learning skills depends on how a surgeon detects, perceives and uses important sensory information. Sources of sensory information particularly important in surgery are visual and kinaesthetic. Vividness and controllability therefore are considered to be the two primary dimensions of imagery.

The processes that occur during cognitive simulation are image generation, observation, maintenance and transformation. Vividness of imagery refers to the generation and observation of the image, while controllability is associated with its maintenance and transformation.

Imagery ability alludes to the content of the image. Vividness and controllability are key aspects in this context. Vividness is the intrinsic characteristics of the image, its clarity and richness, and controllability is the manipulation, transformation and retention of the mental image. The accuracy shows how imagery reflects the reality of the mental content. Besides clarity, vividness is also about sensory richness. It is a measure of the intensity of activity of the cognitive process underlying the imagery, and just how life-like an image appears. Vivid imagery conjures up mental representations with the use of detailed sensory cues. Ideally, such mental simulation is very close to the actual experience of the movement itself, hence simultaneously increasing the exactness of imagery. In technical terms, vividness can be likened to a resolution of a picture quality of a TV: the higher the resolution, the better the image quality.

Controllability is imagery maintenance and modulation, the ease and accuracy with which an image is transformed or manipulated in the mind, and it is a key factor in the mental rotation of a perceptual stimulus. One has to be careful as images can be manipulated easily yet inadequately and the exactness of the imagery may thus be compromised.

People with high vividness and high control show the greatest improvement in performance with the application of imagery techniques. Those with low vividness and high control follow, while those with low vividness and low control come next and, lastly, are those with high vividness and low control. In fact, the last category, high vividness and low control, may be detrimental to performance. Uncontrolled images lead to situations that may have negative consequences. It is therefore important for performers to learn to control their images. Skilled performers seem to have both better control and vividness than those less skilled.

Modalities of cognitive simulation

The word imagery instantly brings to mind the concept of visuals in the 'mind's eye'. However, the most powerful imagery entails the inputs from multiple senses perceived simultaneously or in rapid succession. The use of multiple senses ensures enriched and more effective images, but this is not always easy, as most people prefer to use imagery in one or two senses only. It is estimated that approximately two-thirds of mental images are visual in nature. The ability to switch between imagery modalities is a skill usually seen among high-level performers. Of all the various modalities, the visual and kinaesthetic ones have received the most attention.

Kinaesthetic imagery refers to the sensory information from receptors about body part location and movement, and the movement of muscles, tendons, and joints (137). Kinaesthetic sensation is 'feeling the movement or the feel of the movement'. This involves creating the sensation of how it feels to perform an action, including the force and effort perceived during movement. It also involves the sense of position, balance, muscle tension, gravity and effort. For example, you may imagine how much muscle tension you would use to push your body into the air as you jump, or how much effort you need to stroke ahead through water when you are swimming.

With the five extraceptive senses (sight, taste, smell, touch and hearing) we perceive the outside world and with interoceptive senses we perceive pain and movement of internal organs. Proprioception is the third distinct sensory modality that provides information about our position and movement of our body. Proprioception is made up of two sub systems, i. e., kinaesthetic and vestibular systems. Although these two systems are separate, they are closely co-ordinated in their operation.

Imagery in different modalities elicits specific changes in the brain for the processing of information in the relevant modalities. In the visualisation of a task, the occipital region of the brain registers activity. In the movement imagery of the same task, the activity is in the frontal area and not the occipital cortex. Thus, visual imagery activates visual pathways and kinaesthetic imagery activates motor pathways. Visual and kinaesthetic imagery are distinct modalities, serve different purposes and provide different information in imagery. Both are important and their effectiveness depends on the purpose of imagery and the nature of the task being imagined.

Jacobson's experiments culminated in one that supports the relationship between the nature of imagery modality and the concomitant response. He attached bipolar electrodes to the bicep brachii muscle and a mono-polar electrode to the muscles of the ipsilateral eye. Amplitude measurements were made by a galvanometer. When subjects were instructed to visualise bending their right arm, an increased action potential occurred in the ocular muscles, but was absent in the biceps. Conversely, when subjects were asked to imagine bending the right arm, muscular activity was observed in the biceps while ocular activity was absent (138).

A close match between the sensory modality and the desired result will enhance the benefits of the imagery. A combination of visual and kinaesthetic imagery therefore is an effective approach (139).

One study classified participants as:

1. High visual and high kinaesthetic
2. High visual and low kinaesthetic
3. Low visual and low kinaesthetic imagers

Their results of comparisons of how well the participants learned a skill using imagery showed that the first group, i.e. the high visual and high kinaesthetic imagers were the best learners, while the low visual and low kinaesthetic imagers were at the opposite end (140).

Tactile imagery

Perceptions of touch are of particular importance to the operating surgeon. Just like vision, the human perceptual system has evolved to perceive information through the skin, and not by means of instruments that pass through surgical ports in the body wall of the patient. The skin on the fingertips is most sensitive and is of crucial importance to the surgeon. A surgeon is most acutely aware of the loss of this information when first operating with the endoscope. However, over time the perceptual system will adapt to the degradation of information. This adaptation process may vary between individuals.

A surgeon must be able to identify tissue properties and handle it in an appropriate manner. Haptic feedback could be used to detect small tissue surface irregularities, to regulate forces applied to the tissues to avoid damage, to manipulate delicate tissues, and for greater precision and accuracy in difficult procedures. As we know the distinct disadvantage with image-guided surgical techniques is the considerable diminishing of haptic input that a surgeon must compensate for during the procedure. Lack of haptic feedback is the bane of robotic surgery as well. However, endoscopic instruments do provide some form of haptic feedback that a skilled surgeon can interpret into texture, shape, and consistency.

Tactile imagery is closely related to kinaesthetic imagery: in fact the two can be, and are combined under the tactile-kinaesthetic label. Distinguishing between the two is necessary, since purely kinaesthetic imagery need not be elicited by touch, but is a prerequisite for tactile imagery. The complex haptic perception process could be called as active touch as opposed to a passive touch (141). Brushing up against some object unintentionally is passive touch, while active touch is purposefully examining say, a gall bladder covered by connective tissue, or a pocketful of coins, and discerning size, shape, texture, border and mobility. The exterior of a gall bladder, though covered by connective tissue, can be sensed, and the values of coins in a pocket though unseen, can be estimated. Haptic awareness forms a kind of visualisation, and the visceral cortex is one of the highest centres involved in the processing of tactile information.

Verbal imagery

Verbal imagery or self-talk is conversation with oneself, covert or overt, speaking to oneself about the performance. In the context of performance, the frequency and content of self-talk creates a mindset within which the performer operates. Mindsets created by thinking strategies influence the quality of performance, which is why developing the skills of 'intentional thinking' is advocated. The myriad mindsets created by self-talk fall into polarised categories, such as self-defeating thoughts or self-enhancing thoughts: winners versus losers. It is easy to intuitively imagine the mindsets that different thought patterns create within the performer. The ultimate objective of addressing the content of a performer's self-talk is to develop a process-oriented type of thinking.

What the performer thinks in relation to their performance can have a significant impact. The interplay between the performer's self-talk and imagery influences the triggering of specific motor programmes used in performance. This line of thought entails a vocabulary of trigger words used to facilitate concentration on the task at hand; the formation of appropriate images associated with performance and the proper mindset for performance and the formation of motor programmes.

Olfactory imagery

The sense of smell is all important for animals but much less so for humans. Still olfactory images can be powerful because they have the most direct pathway to the brain than all other sensory images. A smell can instantly conjure up as a flashback the distinct ambience of a place visited long ago. Smell attracts and repels humans like no other sensory stimulation. Though the olfactory sense may not be of practical significance in cognitive simulation, it is a barometer for the quality of imagery and ability. Some surgeons describing the imagery of an operation will mention the smell of burnt tissue after the (imaginary) use of cautery.

Perspectives of cognitive simulation

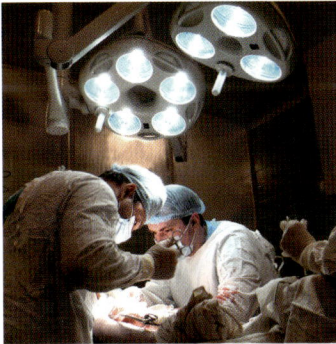

External

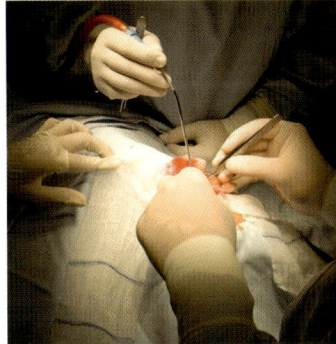

Internal

The two different approaches in imagining a movement are, visualisation with the 'interior view' or by producing a 'mental video'. The first type of imagery is called internal perspective and the second, external perspective. External perspective means watching one's own body executing a skill as if watching oneself in a video recording: someone videotaping an operation you are performing with the camera focused on you .

An internal perspective is creating a visual image, like looking through one's own eyes and simultaneously feeling the muscular contractions and sensations that occur during actual movement. The image is much more vivid, as not only do you see everything happen - through your own eyes and not the camera eye – but you can also feel and touch the equipment with your hands, and there may be even the sound of machines during the operation.

An external perspective is most common in the initial stages of learning a skill, particularly if it is a closed task, i.e. self-paced and predominantly under the control of the performer. An internal perspective is used to imagine well-learnt skills.

Both perspectives are extremely useful in skill development.

The benefits of external perspective are:

1. It is possible to move your perspective around and see the action from various positions (not available to the internal perspective) so you can analyse different aspects of the technique.

2. It can be used even if the task has not been executed before.

3. It may be primarily helpful when learning a new skill (especially by demonstration) or when you are trying to isolate and correct mistakes in skill execution.

The benefits of internal perspective are -

1. A more realistic experience of the actual movement, providing identical perceptual information - you see the surroundings as if they were actually there and you feel the movements as if executing them.

2. It may offer more potential for performance benefits, because it has the potential to use all the senses and therefore should aid the transfer of training to actual performance.

3. It can be rehearsed by performers to practise procedure strategies, rehearse recognition of visual and kinaesthetic cues, identify and correct kinaesthetic movement problems and cope with debilitating performance anxiety.

Some say internal imagery is more effective than external imagery for enhancing performance, especially in procedures that have been performed repeatedly. Jacobson was the first to prove that internal imagery involves more muscle activity than external imagery. Eye activity occurred in subjects thinking of performing a bicep curl (external imagery). In imagining a bicep curl (internal imagery), localised muscle activity took place. Internal imagery is also known to produce greater somatic arousal and less visual activity than external imagery.

The value of internal or external orientation could depend on the individual's level of experience with cognitive simulation. There are benefits to be gained from switching perspectives: just as visual and kinaesthetic imagery refer to different sources of information, internal and external imagery also refer to different sources of information and a first person or third person perspective.

Temporal aspect of cognitive simulation

Time is also a valid factor en route to successful imagery. The transit time for an imagined walk and (mental) arrival at a specific destination is remarkably similar to the actual time taken to physically walk that distance (102). The interest in imagery speed manipulation is of recent origin. Kosslyn in his renowned study used an image-scanning paradigm to prove that more time was required to scan longer distances mentally (142). Similar temporal equivalence has been established through a large variety of motor tasks regarding motor imagery *per se*, proving that changing motor imagery speeds is sufficient to elicit changes in the timing of actual movement (143). This conclusion can be used to improve the speed of actions. At times even if actions become habitual and smooth, the performance remains slower than expected. In view of the imagery and real time equivalence, faster imagery time would speed up the movements.

One can also use slow motion imagery for each component to help participants see each part clearly. This imagery technique can be particularly useful while learning a skill. Slow motion replays of a task can give a clearer picture of its progression and can also be a boon in high-speed skills that are to be completed in a second or two. Important bodily cues or components such as a particular arm position can be easily identified and practised through slow motion imagery.

Slow motion imagery could prove difficult at first but does improve with practice. However, as the normal execution is at real speed, the maximum benefits cannot be transferred from practice to performance by over emphasising slow motion imagery. It is best to conclude a session with normal speed imagery so that the mental rehearsal speed matches actual performance, and hence maximises the transfer of practice.

Positioning for cognitive simulation

The recommendation is to adopt a relaxed position in the initial days of an imagery training. Being at rest when using imagery means not reinforcing habitual patterns of movement. Being relaxed is conducive to being focused in imagery experience, thanks to reduced somatic tension and the elimination of distractions. Relaxed position sets the stage for the production of vivid images.

However some people argue that relaxation could have a negative impact on performance as it inhibits the possible transfer effects of practice; the individual will not be relaxed during the actual performance so relaxed imagery practice may actually be detrimental to the impending performance. Thus, a pragmatic approach would be to adopt a relaxed posture only in the beginning of the imagery. Relaxation before imagery practice ensures it is more vivid and better controlled, which in turn makes it more effective. The aim is not to keep the subject totally relaxed throughout mental practice, but to use relaxation to induce vivid imagery.

As such, imagery can be practiced in a various situations or positions such as sitting, walking or while waiting for the patient to be brought to the operating theatre. There is much to be gained by using imagery during other everyday movements,this also means a constructive use of unproductive time

In some cases, bringing the body into a position similar to the task and moving slightly helps in the generation of a motor image. Imagery is generally performed *sans* movement in the interest of improving performance, but there are advantages in performing imagery while moving slightly, or in positioning that relates to the target movement.

Cognitive simulation script

The content of the imagery is a crucial factor in its practice. Cognitive simulation is like installing a program into the human body as if into a computer drive. The outcome then will reflect the programming quality. If what is practised through imagery is incorrect, the eventual performance will in all likelihood be inadequate. Correct practice makes perfect while incorrect practice makes for imperfection. Careful planning of the content of imagery will maximise its effects in the effective acquisition of imagery skill. Ideally, surgeons could write their own imagery script to be used for a procedure.

For the maximum benefits from imagery the individual needs to be conversant with the procedure. To gain familiarity, imagery scripts must lay emphasis on underpinning the imagery representation of the skill. Such a script typically includes thorough directions on how to perform a procedure and also clues from diverse sensory modalities that enhance the experience. The aim is to facilitate a precise mental representation of the skill that is to be improved. Some of these are visual cues, kinaesthetic cues and cognitive cues. For example, task-relevant thoughts that go through the mind while performing the procedure. It is widely believed that movement-related kinaesthetic sensation plays a major role in imagery instructions. The kinaesthetic aspects of imagery, for instance, call for a focus on how the hands or fingers feel during movement or imagined movement to facilitate kinaesthetic sensations.

Some studies on imagery have shown conflicting results. With poorly reported instructions for imagery, the benefits of differing perspectives adopted during the process remain nebulous. Factors that could be responsible for this variability include the nature of the instructions and the variability of individuals in conducting imagery. Unclear or ambiguous imagery instructions may cause the content of the image to differ, significantly compromising the similarity with the physical task, and therefore the predicted development of the skill.

Writing an imagery script

Writing an imagery script can be seen as a three-step process.

Step one - Core content: outline the basic content of the procedure or situation to be imagined. Write it in the first person (I) if it is being used for yourself or the second person (you) if it is to be read to someone else. In describing how a skill is executed, ensure all components are included as well as the correct behaviour emphasised, especially if it is complex in nature.

Step two - The details and sensory stimuli: descriptors (adjectives) that add colour, detail and movement (for example – the speed of the movement) to the original script components or events. Add movements or kinaesthetic feelings, body responses and emotional responses.

Step three - Refining the script: you may want to re-write components or actions into a paragraph that can be read easily and clearly. Re-read it and try to imagine the event in all its sensory, action and emotional details. Do you feel as if you are actually executing the skill or experiencing the event? If not, re-examine the description to see if it accurately reflects the sensations associated with this action.

To provide a template, an example of cognitive simulation script is provided in the appendix at the end of the book.

Given that imagery is a technique like any other, a number of factors can influence its effectiveness.

Here are some of the relevant factors:

1. Nature of the task – It is reasonable to assume that the learning and performance of all tasks will not benefit equally from cognitive simulation. Some procedures are likely to lend themselves more to imagery than others. Different movements or steps in a procedure can have different imagery values, i.e. a rating of how easily the movement can be imagined. The easier the movement pattern is to imagine, the better it is remembered (144). Therefore, when learning a task, some consideration should be given to how easy the task is to imagine. If it is somewhat difficult to image, alternative techniques to help to acquire the skill, such as verbal descriptions, may be useful.

2. Cognitive versus motor skills - The cognitive component in a performance has been linked with the benefits of imagery rehearsal. A meta-analysis states that the size of effect produced by imagery was larger for cognitive tasks compared to manual tasks. Tasks that are very cognitive in nature benefit from imagery more than tasks that involve pure motor skills. However, the cognitive dimension of a task changes as the skill level of a performer changes. A novice may be thinking about how to accomplish a skill, while an expert is concentrating on the strategy techniques and tactics related to performing it. As far a surgical procedures are concerned, It is pragmatic to view them on a cognitive - motor continuum and not divide them rigidly into mutually exclusive categories.

3. Imagery instructions - Since imagery is a multi-dimensional process, the instructions to a performer are important. They must contain sufficient detail to ensure that the performer is imaging the task in the desired manner. It is also useful to include the performance outcome in the instructions.

4. Skill level – Is imagery more useful for a beginner or an expert? There are contrasting views. Some argue that imagery is more advantageous to beginners. This is founded on the basis that the early phase of learning is mostly cognitive, and we have seen that imagery facilitates the execution of the cognitive components.

The other opinion claims that imagery will be of the most benefit when the performer is acquainted with the task, as it ensures that a robust representation of the skill is created in the mind. Experience helps the performer to form a precise image of what an ideal performance should be. Successive performance then aims at simulating the imaged performance.

More recent studies conclude that imagery helps both the novice as well as skilled performers for different reasons. It is probably appropriate then to encourage performers at all skill levels to use cognitive simulation. The manner in which the imagery instructions are framed for these levels, however, might differ widely. Novices are developing basic skills, and so their imagery instructions will emphasise imagining themselves performing these skills correctly. For skilled performers imagery might be acting more as a means of reinforcement. They are more likely to use imagery for strategy development and controlling arousal levels.

5. Imagery ability - The imagery ability of performers should be an important variable to consider. It seems reasonable to assume that with individuals low in imagery ability, imagery will have little or no effect.

6. Positive versus negative imagery - Performers should image themselves performing accurately and successfully. Not imaging a positive outcome or not imaging the skill correctly will affect its proper acquisition and execution. This is important because positive or accurate imagery enhances subsequent performance, whereas negative or imperfect imagery results in impaired performance.

7. Types of skill – There are open skills and closed skills. Open skills are those for which the environment or the situation is constantly changing so that the performer cannot effectively plan a response. In such situations it is difficult to conduct imagery. Open skills do not seem, intuitively, to be open to mental rehearsal. Closed skills, on the other hand, are where the environment is predictable. The use of imagery is therefore more easily applied to a closed, repetitive skill performed virtually the same way every time.

For some readers the intricate information provided so far about cognitive simulation may seem to be overly complicated. Well, think of it as a reminder that the mind can and does perform these and a myriad other feats frequently without we becoming aware of it. The point is to become aware of what the mind can do and practise cognitive simulation in all its variations to turn inherent mental ability into a tool to improve surgical performance.

Key points

- Cognitive simulation is a skill which needs to be developed like any other skill.

- Understanding the factors which makes cognitive simulation effective will help to develop the skills.

- Dimensions, modalities and perspectives are the fundamental features that needs to be considered in imagery development.

- Involving various senses especially kinaesthetic and visual and appropriate use of internal/external perspective are the key factors for imagery quality.

- Careful planning of the content of imagery script will maximise its effects in the effective acquisition.

Chapter 7

Cognitive simulation training

Imagine entering a dark room with a torch. If you point the torch beam in one direction, you see a coffee table. Turn the beam in another direction, and a TV set and sofa can be seen. Well, what the narrow torch actually lights up are just parts of the objects, such as the legs of the table or parts of the TV set and sofa. It is the brain that fills in the unseen parts of the objects lit up by the torch and enables their identification as table, TV set and sofa.

Now replace the narrow torch beam by a laser beam that is far narrower, just a little dot of light that provides minimal data to identify the objects. This would be an appropriate representation of how limited our senses are at receiving information from the outside world. Continuing the torch analogy, as the person walks through the dark room, he may then become aware of subtle sounds, hints of light or the feel of the floor under his feet. In this way additional sensory gateways are opened, to increase the input of sensory information. Turning up the 'volume' of the relevant sensory perceptions is a key ingredient in improving a motor skill. Usually when we are standing, the focus is not necessarily on the distribution of pressure on the feet. By turning up the volume on tactile perception, the extra information may be used to adjust the balance between the feet. Turning up the volume on sensations of hands or finger movements will enable the skill of imagining movement kinaesthetically to improve. The impact of cognitive simulation is in direct proportion to the development or fine-tuning of the information gathering capacities of the senses. Just like a master painter who can distinguish between the subtlest of hues and shades, sensory images should be viewed with judicious discretion.

To derive maximum benefits from cognitive simulation, the approach must be effective. An inappropriate application may lead to the conclusion that it does not work. An image that flickers like a candle in the wind is far less effective than one that is steady and long lasting. The ability to transform an image is an invaluable asset in getting to the goals of movement. Here again, the ability to manipulate images is indispensable. Practice will ensure a familiarity with the many approaches in the learning of the most effective and constructive use of cognitive simulation.

Imagery practice and the development of surgical skills

John Hall, The American Journal of Surgery 2002 (145)

An imagery program should be designed to facilitate the use of imagery. The objective would be to incorporate imagery into daily routine, both within the operating theatre as well as outside. It should include:

The development of self-awareness in surgeons about their use of imagery

The quantification of imagery abilities

The application of imagery as a tool to be used in day-to-day practice

Personal debriefing aimed at identifying problems through self-evaluation

This approach should take the skill learning towards a mentally active process rather than 'skill-learning by osmosis'.

Stages of imagery practice:

1. Task definition
2. Prior learning
3. Mental rehearsal
4. Reflection
5. Problem solving
6. Reality check

It is important to start with a clear concept of the task at hand and then accumulate enough practical experience to make useful practice possible. In practice, these steps usually occur in an opportunistic manner, but there are benefits in adopting a more formal approach.

Training

Cognitive simulation training can be offered in an individual or a group format. The goals, the rate of absorbing new information and the experience of the surgeon will determine how long the training would be required. Imagery training must be imparted in a systematic manner if it is to be effective. Ideally it should be practised for at least 10-15 minutes daily until the competency is achieved. Alternating between actual procedures and imagery practice will optimise imagery benefits. Some anecdotal reports indicate that a good time for imagery practice is just before going to sleep. A mental rehearsal of the goals to be attained just before going to bed will help in recreating stronger and clearer images when one is awake (146). Imagery practice must be long enough to facilitate easy flowing response, but care should be taken to avert any diminishing of interest. A quiet place could be used initially but for the later practice the operation theatre could be used.

The following section contains exercises designed to illuminate ways to develop cognitive simulation skills. It is useful to assess the current level of imagery skill before embarking on an improvement course.

Preliminary assessment

The generic exercise that follows will help in the assessment of general imagery skills. All that is required is a quiet environment, which is conducive to concentration with no distraction or disturbance. Stop at the end of each instruction, close your eyes and attempt the imagery.

- Imagine a bowl of fruit.
- Imagine the colours, yellow bananas, green and red apples, oranges, juicy green grapes, and multi-hued pineapples.
- Imagine picking up an orange.
- Feel the surface of the orange with your fingers.

- See the juice squirt out as your fingernails puncture the orange skin.
- Imagine the smell of the orange as you peel it.
- Imagine the sound as you clean the white pith and separate the segments.
- Feel the sticky juice run on to your fingers.
- Imagine the taste and feel of the orange on your tongue as your teeth bite into a segment.

Answer the following questions:

1. Were you able to create the images?
   Very easily / Easily / A little / Hardly at all / Not at all

2. Could you sustain the images?
   Very easily / Easily / A little / Hardly at all / Not at all

3. Which sense did you find easiest to imagine?
   Sight / Sound / Smell / Touch / Taste

4. Which was the most difficult to conjure up?
   Sight / Sound / Smell / Touch / Taste

5. Did you use internal or external imagery?
   Internal / External / Combination

Outlined below are exercises in surgical settings.

Create a global profile of your imagery skills to determine strengths and weaknesses and to select the appropriate exercise to help in the application of skills. Consider all aspects of imagery: internal, external, clarity, control, speed, duration, perspective and the use of the five senses. Rate yourself on a scale of 1 to 10 on each aspect by marking the segment. Focus on the greatest discrepancies and relative weaknesses, and determine the aspects of imagery most relevant to those elements of performance, which in turn will help you zero in on the appropriate exercise to enhance your practising abilities.

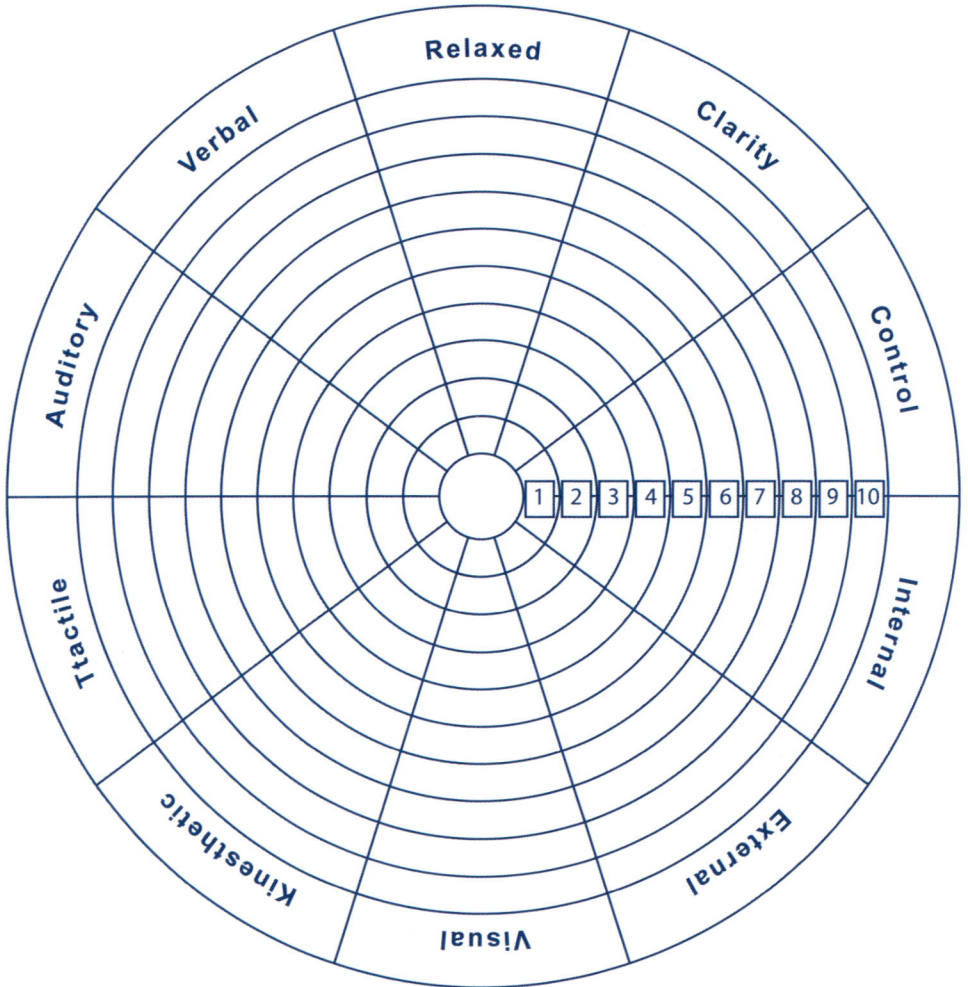

Exercise 1

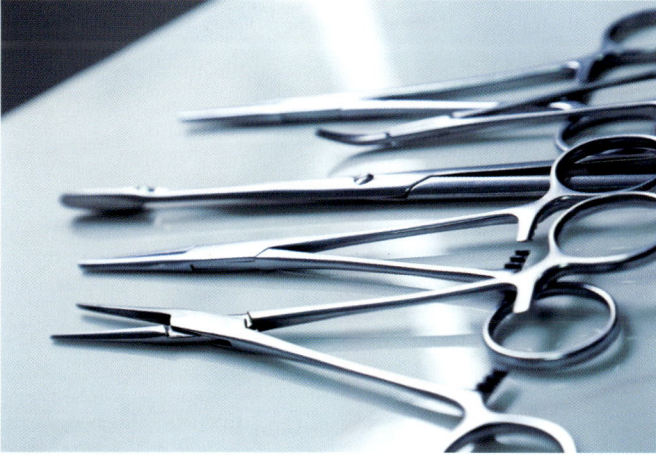

Select a surgical instrument. Scrutinise it in detail, the colour, design, shape, insignia, brand logo etc. Close your eyes and imagine the instrument in all its intricate detail.

Rate your experience on the visual analogue scale.

1 10

Could not see anything   Vividly and accurately

Repeat the exercise, observing the instrument in detail, and then recreating it mentally in the minutest detail. Then evaluate the improvement in visual imagery.

See every image with a fresh perspective, as if you have never seen it before. Unless you let go of a previous experience, it is not possible to have a new one.

Exercise 2

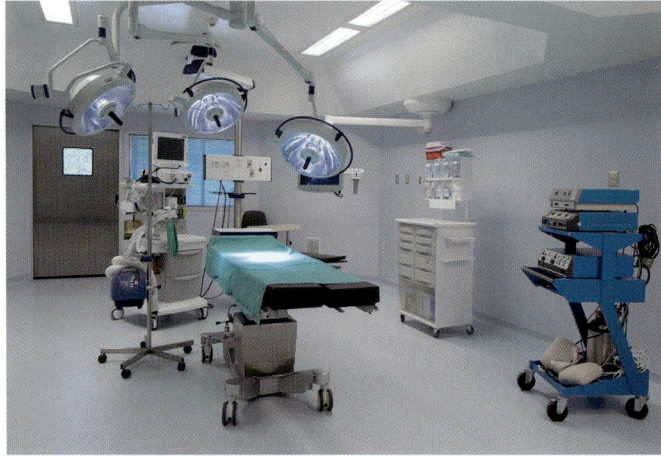

Visualise an operating theatre with your eyes closed. Imagine its layout, the walls, floor, ceiling, lights, operating table and other equipment, the anaesthetist, nurses and ancillary staff. Imagine the sounds of the monitors, suction machine etc.

Rate how accurately and effectively you conjured up the theatre environs.

1 10

Could not experience anything   Vividly and accurately

Some individuals are able to monitor the quality of their experience while performing the imagery. This meta-imagistic function can improve the quality of the imagery but one also needs to be aware that the additional mental activity can disturb the process, and reduce its clarity and effectiveness.

Exercise 3

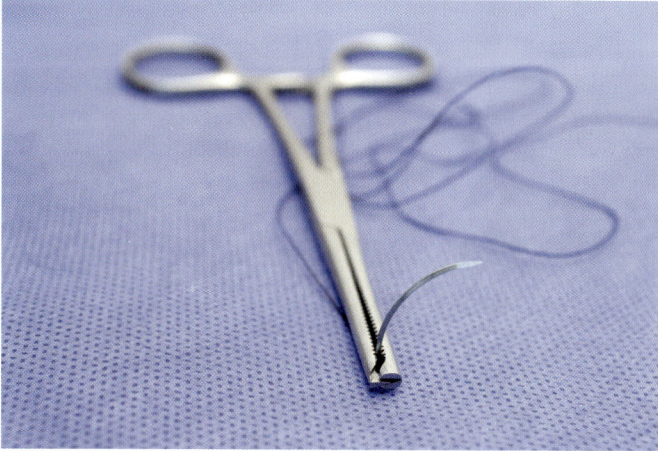

Take a surgical instrument. Focus on its feel and the differences in texture. Close your eyes because the shutdown of one's predominant sense, vision, can enhance tactile imagery.

Put it away and try to recall its texture and feel.

Experiment with different instruments, several times, handling the instruments and then recreating their feel mentally.

Rate the vividness of the imagery on a 10-point scale.

1 10

Could not feel anything   Vividly and accurately

Invest adequate and uninterrupted time focusing on each image. Inadequate concentration will result in vague and inadequate memory recall as well as inconsistent execution. In contrast, dwelling too long on the same instrument is likely to cause boredom and fatigue, which can in turn mean diminished concentration and performance.

Exercise 4

Take a relatively simple skill to practise kinaesthetic imagery, such as tying a surgical knot. Execute the movement physically, with or without the actual material. Close your eyes and execute the movement mentally.

Focus on the kinaesthetic feelings in the parts of your hands executing the skill. Look where you normally look during the action, and be aware of how your fingers and hands move.

Rate how accurately you captured the feel of the movement.

1 10

Could not feel the movement   Vividly and accurately

Closing the eyes and focusing on the relevant body parts during movement improves kinaesthetic ability.

Those not very proficient in kinaesthetic imagery could start with sensations of simple movements like lifting the arms above the head, lowering them and remembering the feeling of this action. Or step forward, then back and recall the feeling during the movement.

First attempt a skill physically to develop kinaesthetic awareness. For this purpose, the best time to mentally rehearse a skill is immediately after it has been executed. After performance, stop briefly and replay the visual and kinaesthetic aspects of the skill in the mind. Such repetition helps in establishing the appropriate neuromuscular circuits in the memory.

Combine observation with imagery. Watch your own or others' best performances to create optimal imagery. This will speed up the process. After watching the performance of a challenging procedure, try to imitate the manoeuvres with all the kinaesthetic astuteness you possess.

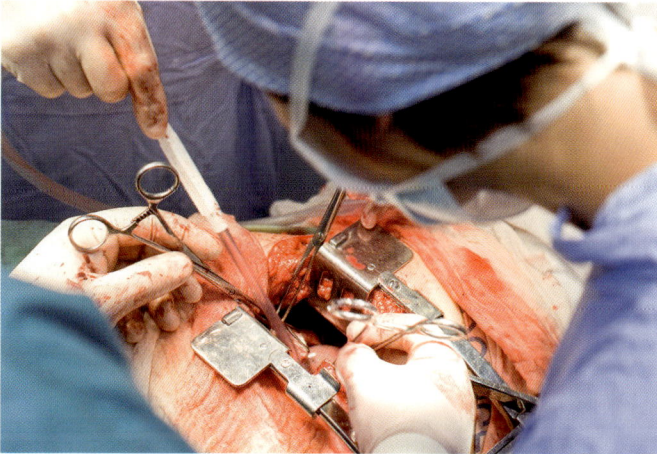

Exercise 5

Watch another surgeon perform a procedure, and focus on specific components of his action. Imagine what this skill component clearly looks like from an external perspective. Focus first on the visual action, then close your eyes and focus on the movement sensation.

Exercise 6

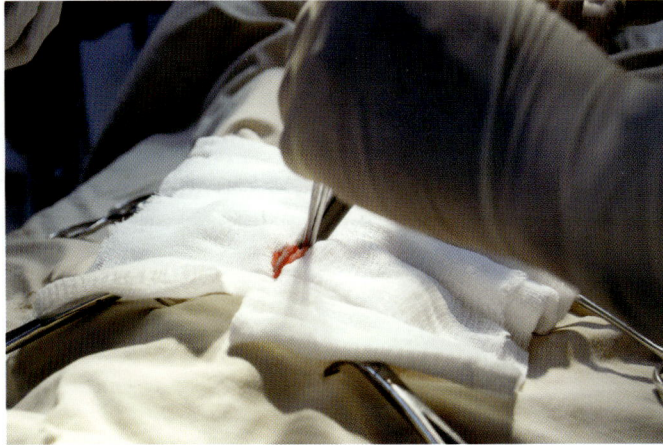

Select a skill, technique or a component of procedure. View your own performance either by remembering the procedure, or by recording your own performance.

When you begin to feel the kinaesthetic sensation of the action, close your eyes and imagine seeing the movement and feeling the sensation of the movement. Visualise from an internal viewpoint and feel the movements of the technique. To develop a more powerful visual aid for internal visualisation, try to record the procedure from an internal perspective. Use a hand held camera to film the task to record the same cues you would normally see. This videotaped internal perspective helps in the generation of the kinaesthetic feeling that accompanies the movement. View this internal recording, then close your eyes, and imagining the same perspective and feeling the sensation of movement occurs more easily.

Exercise 7

Both external and internal imagery can be very powerful tools. Learn to use both and to switch from one to the other. To practise external imagery, choose a skill and view a video recording of yourself. Then close your eyes and try to visualise the entire sequence from the same external perspective. Subsequently, visualise the technique from an internal perspective during its execution. Switch from the internal to external perspective and back, and observe which works better for you.

Exercise 8

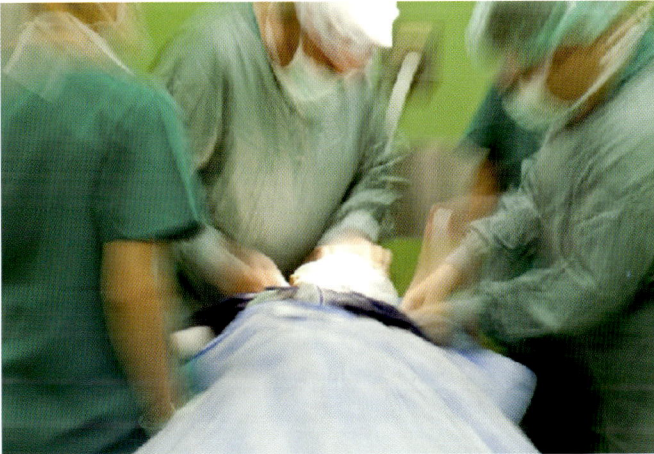

Strategies can be employed to maximise the effectiveness of imagery. To exercise control over the image, break down the skill into smaller components (segmenting) to be able to see each part lucidly. Slow down the imagery for each component to perceive each part clearly. This is particularly useful when first learning a skill. Slow motion replays of a task give you a clearer picture of its progression. Slow motion imagery is a big boon for high-speed skills, but remember over-emphasis on slow motion imagery in practice will not ensure the maximum benefits at the normal execution speed. So, conclude the imagery session with normal speed imagery to enable mental rehearsal speed to match the movement speed, which in turn will maximise the transfer of training.

Exercise 9

To control speed and duration, select a basic technique. It should ideally be a fairly closed and discrete skill, i.e. one with a clear beginning and end, one that can be executed without too much influence from outside factors.

Imagine executing the task as you have just performed it - from an internal perspective. Close your eyes, and start a stopwatch as you begin imaging the action and stop it when you have completed it. Compare the times taken to execute the technique physically, and for its imagery execution. If too slow, speed up the imagery processing and reduce time spent on the different components. With repetition, the imagery time will get closer and closer to the actual execution time.

Exercise 10

This exercise in error correction also helps in switching from one perspective to another (external and internal). Use external imagery to replay a problematic technique and try to determine where the difficulty lies. Rehearse the technique and observe what you are doing correctly. Note when and where errors creep in. Employ demonstrations or video recordings of other surgeons to evaluate your own execution. After identifying the problem, use kinaesthetic based internal imagery to feel what the movement is like when it is incorrect and when it is correct.

To control the image and therefore the outcome of the action, break down the skill in the imagery exercise into smaller components (segmenting) to visualise each section clearly.

A video camera is a handy tool to enhance imagery training ability as visual aids improve vividness and control. While learning a new skill there is only a hazy picture of the task component, so viewing it over and over again will help create a clear memory imprint. Slow motion playbacks help in acquiring the correct technique more quickly, and to gain a clear picture of the task. Start imagery at slow speeds and graduate to a real time pace. This also brings awareness of any errors and subsequently aids in their elimination. Visual aids are particularly useful to set right recurrent errors in technique or form, and video recordings from an outside perspective (external) will help pinpoint continuing problems. During external imagery rehearsal, the rectification of errors and a flawless performance can be visualised.

Key points

■ Practice will ensure a familiarity with the many approaches in learning the most effective use of cognitive simulation.

■ You may think of 4 Rs in relation to cognitive simulation training. They stand for relaxation, realism, regularity and reinforcement. To spell it out, a relaxed state is conducive to producing vivid images. Realism means conjuring up imagery as real as actually executing the skill. Clarity, vividness and control are key factors in invoking the most realistic imagery. Practice also must be regular for optimum benefits. Reinforcement implies using visual or kinaesthetic aids to enhance the quality and control of imagery.

■ To comply with the principles and maximise the effectiveness of imagery, the following points are relevant:
1. Employ imagery for skill development and maintenance, and to strengthen the qualities necessary for performance.
2. Practise imagery for use in specific situations, such as immediately before the procedure, after the procedure, at critical points and after an error. These images would include the repeated rehearsal of complex skills, strategies and the enhancement of other psychological skills.
3. Once basic imagery skills have been adequately developed, revise the imagery script to upgrade the level of performance.

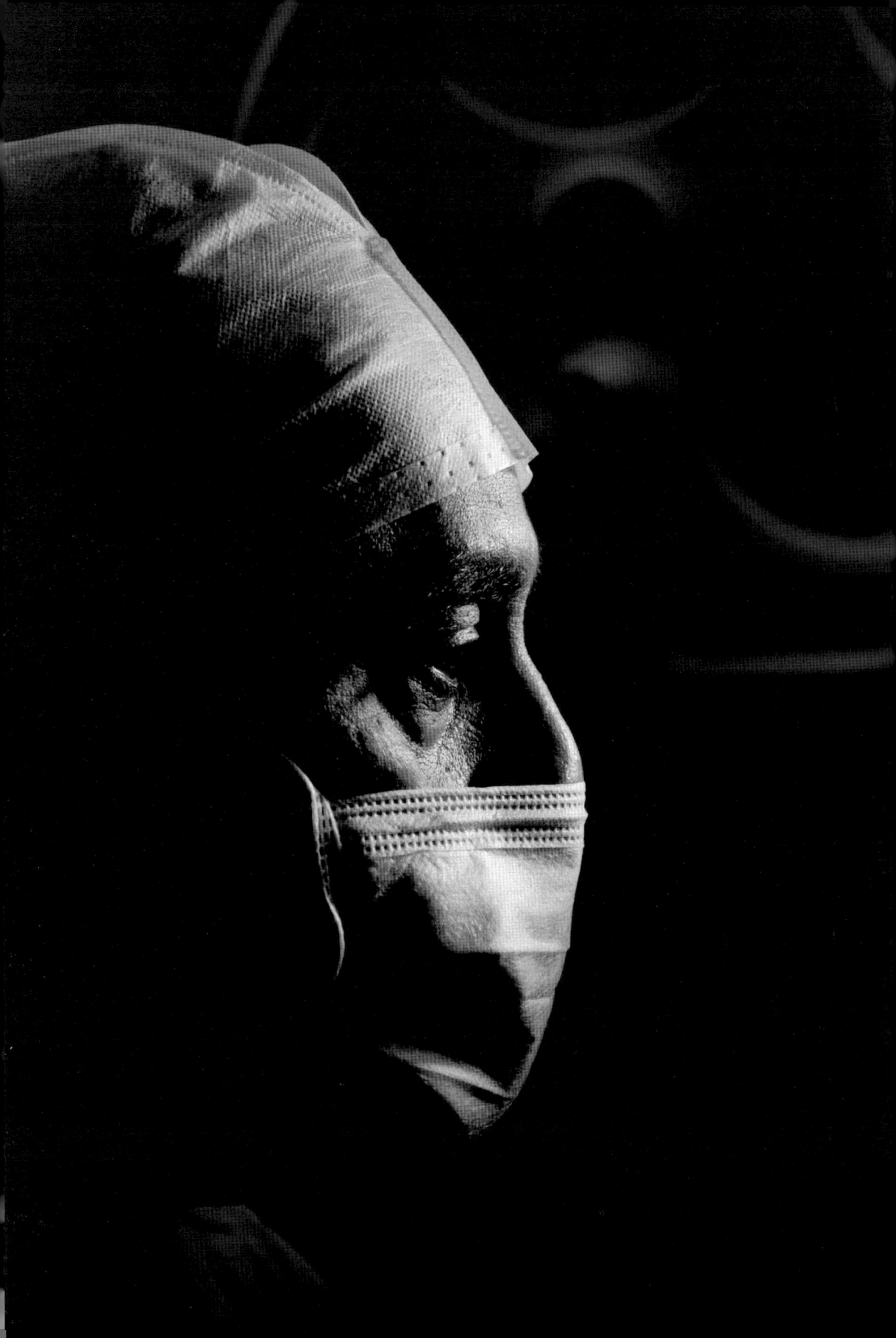

Chapter 8

Applications of cognitive simulations

Cognitive simulation, in a broad sense, is like computer software, but a version designed for the human mind. It is a technique that programmes the mind to respond in a certain manner. No physical props or outside stimulus are necessary, as it is an activity that can be engaged in while seated in a chair. Imagine a movement, and the experience in the mind's eye can be as vivid as it is when doing it for real. During intense and vivid imagery, the brain perceives and interprets images as being real. That is why cognitive simulation has immense potential and scope to be a boon and a blessing in the surgical arena. However, it is only as valuable as its proper application. Its applications is influenced by a number of variables, primarily the various goals the surgeon seeks to achieve through its use to enhance performance. Cognitive simulation perforce has a wide range of applications in surgical practice.

A. Acquiring skills

Cognitive simulation can be applied to skill learning in all three stages, namely, cognitive, associative and automatic. The cognitive stage involves working out actions that are usually implicit, to make them explicit. For example, it will help an inexperienced trainee to focus on just what is involved in the insertion of a trocar for a laparoscopic procedure. A trainee with more experience could review the various stages of such an operation, which he has previously only observed. An experienced surgeon meanwhile may rehearse the variations that could occur in the course of a more complicated presentation.

Cognitive simulation could be applied to a review of anatomy as it can help surgeons become oriented in complex anatomic areas. Accurate mental representations of structures in the vicinity of a dissection will ensure more efficient planning of manoeuvres. Trainees should be encouraged to form mental images as they observe procedures. Such images can consist of visible anatomy but also and perhaps more importantly, of structures not yet exposed. As learning evolves to the stage of automation, cognitive simulation assumes a form of risk management. To elaborate, while a novice will be concerned with what to do next to complete a procedure, an expert surgeon only thinks about key steps of operations, even in case of rare or complex operations.

B. Shortening the learning curve

It is important to recognise cognitive approaches to minimise the learning curve of surgical procedures. Too much emphasis is given on the volume of operative experience, rather than the quality of learning experience. Of what use are log book entries of operations unless they are complimented by active learning processes?(147) Indeed, methods of teaching surgical skills outside operating theatres are interesting but their nature and the extent of their usefulness is not well known. In particular, there is a need for programmes following workshops to maximise skill retention and advancement. This can be fulfilled by cognitive simulation.

Understanding the learning curve is beneficial in the context of surgical performance, being relevant to both trainees and experienced surgeons exploring novel techniques. We are aware of the basic fact that performance improves with experience and a graph of performance versus experience creates a curve rather than a straight line. Surgeons who are not experienced in performing a particular procedure are said to be in the early phase of the learning curve.

A learning curve has four key stages. The starting co-ordinate 'A' represents the beginning of training. The ascending graph suggests how speedily the individual's performance advances. This section of the curve may be a step-wise climb as the performer acquires steps of a complicated procedure. Progress in performance tends to be speedy initially, before tapering off. With the appropriate aptitude, a stage arrives when the procedure can be performed competently (co-ordinate B). Further practice improves results by a small degree (co-ordinate C), until a plateau is reached (co-ordinate D). As one gets older, manual dexterity, eyesight and cognition start declining. Ageing processes offset any benefit resulting from experience, which may cause a drop in the quality of performance (co-ordinate E). Although not shown in this graph, the learning curve also shows temporary deterioration in performance after competence has been accomplished. The explanations are thought to be a case-mix effect, accepting problematic cases or over-confidence, which cause lapses in technique or judgement (148).

Procedures and predicted number of cases to achieve plateau

1. Laparoscopic fundoplication – 20 cases (149).
2. Laparoscopic colorectal surgery – 80 cases (150).
3. Gastrectomy – 55 cases (151).
4. Oesophagectomy – 150 cases (152).

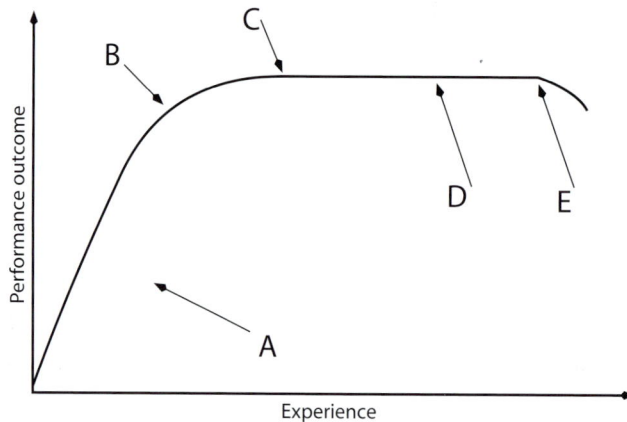

Difficult procedures are sometimes wrongly described to have a steep learning curve. Steepness suggests significant improvements in results are attained in the early stage, and proficiency (co-ordinate B) is accomplished after comparatively short practice. The truth is, complicated procedures have gradual learning curves, in which little improvements occurs with every case, so that co-ordinate B is reached after extensive experience (153). In hiking terminologies, steepness means difficulty. Conversely, steepness can also signify rapid ascent. So, a 'steep learning curve' suggests that skills are acquired quickly since the procedure is relatively simple, or the surgeon is exceptionally dexterous.

To carry the notion further, cognitive simulation could be said to make a surgeon's learning curve steeper. Its use could strengthen an existing skill to the point where it becomes second nature. Once a skill is learned, simulation can reinforce the movements of the skill and give them fluidity and smoothness. Without fluidity in mental performance how can there be fluidity in actual performance?

C. Maintaining the level of skill

Could cognitive simulation be used to perfect an existing skill? In this latter stage, it can be assumed that a clear template of the skill exists. The surgeon already knows how to execute the appropriate movement: the goal now is to increase the chances of perfectly executed movements whenever required. Top-level sportsmen are known to use imagery to enhance their skills. For elite performers, the positive effect of imagery may relate to maximising the transfer of skills from experience to actual performance. Cognitive simulation may enhance a novice's skills by reinforcing a template of the task. At higher skill levels, it serve to enhance efficiency by strengthening the cognitive template. It also maximise the cognitive focus of the performer by improving concentration and reducing skill disruptive levels of arousal. At expert levels of performance, the skill level may well be close to a ceiling effect, leaving little room for actual skill enhancement. Thus, the value of cognitive simulation for top-level performers may mostly lie in ensuring the transfer of skills to actual performance.

D. Providing variety to practice

Cognitive simulation can be used to bring variety to practice when it becomes physically monotonous or unyielding. It can also be of help in improving the performance of a specific part of a procedure. There is a distinction between imagery that focuses on a specific movement, and imagery that is aimed at improving efficiency in general. Specific imagery focuses on improving defined movement skills, while general imagery focuses on rehearsing strategic plans.

E. Transferring skills from an established technique

Cognitive simulation may even be of help in transferring skills from an established technique to a new but closely related task. For example, a surgeon may adopt a minimal access approach to a procedure that has previously been performed by an open approach. For these experienced performers inner reflection and imagery practice may prompt an altered approach.

F. Hindering the decay of skills

Individual physical ability drops with increasing age. Initially, advancing age is complemented by increased wisdom but eventually even mentation declines. First to wane is strength, then vision, agility, and lastly cognition. Knowledge, experience and reputation can compensate for a long time, and the decline is gradual so the surgeon or his colleagues may not notice the changes until the deficits become glaringly serious. Increasing age makes difficult surgery even more so and risky surgery riskier (154). Surgeons over 45 years of age have increased rates of recurrence in laparoscopic hernia repairs (155). A survey of 563 knee replacement patients proved that the rate of surgical complications correlated with the surgeon's age: the younger the surgeon's age, the fewer the complications (156).

Only Wine and Cheese Improve With Age!

At a reputed hospital, a renowned senior surgeon did not evolve from open abdominal surgery to laparoscopic surgery. However, he continued performing laparoscopic procedures. Unfortunately his incapacities had lethal consequences. A patient bled to death during an elective cholecystectomy. Inquiry exposed that for the past few years the staff had regularly been requesting extra blood for this surgeon's procedures, since they were aware that too much bleeding occurred during his procedures. What's more, even the anaesthetists had been usually changing their timetables so as to put an expert anaesthetist for this surgeon's list as they recognised that his surgical risks were far higher. However, no one had ever made the surgeon aware of his deficiency or brought it to the notice of hospital officials. Their reverence for this icon of surgical education was so great that it took a patient's death to be shattered.

There is therefore the requirement to retain old skills, develop new ones, and evolve through experience. Experience is a handy and valid substitute for some mechanical skills though. The deterioration of purely physical skills begins near the end of the third decade of life, at the age of 28 or thereabouts. Cognitive skills diminish later. Most surgeons reach their peak of performance around the second half of their fifth decade, at 45–50 years of age. It is clear then that for more than two decades, the accumulating experience can and does more than compensate for diminishing physical skills.

The potential of cognitive simulation as an aid to maintain skills is well understood by elite musicians. Renowned concert pianist Glenn Gould practised very little physically in the latter part of his career, relying almost exclusively on mental rehearsal (157).

G. Acquiring and practising strategies

Cognitive simulation can be employed when learning new strategies in performance. After the strategies are demonstrated, the performer imagines their execution. The mental experience of pressure situations can prepare one to handle the same situations in real life effectively.

H. Examining performance problems

Cognitive simulation goes well beyond mere intellectual activity, the thinking about or attempting to recall an event. When the action scene is 'switched on', the details of the event are activated. Unlike a movie experience, the performer is not just sitting and watching, but is actually experiencing the event. Cognitive simulation becomes a type of instant replay, enabling the performer to closely attend to what was happening. An application of this phenomenon is for the re-experiencing of a procedure that has gone wrong. Surgeons usually have their own take on what transpired during the difficult procedures, and some will be adamant about the accuracy of their recall, until shown a video replay.

A surgeon can scrutinise his below par performance by means of cognitive simulation to determine and detect the potentially confounding factor. He can then focus on why the error occurred and what could have been done to prevent it. It is important for him then to re-visualise the experience and substitute the correct response.

I. Performance related use of Imagery

Cognitive simulation can also find an application in preparations for actual surgical procedure. Getting to grips with the technique in a laboratory or on a simulator both fail to replicate the conditions of the operating theatre environment. This is where the capacity of cognitive simulation to conjure up real life conditions proves to be of immense value.

The skills a surgeon acquire have practical implications, which means they are to be performed in real time and in the real world. Practice is the preparation, and performance is the execution of what has been learned. A conscious focus is necessary for a beginner to improve a skill that is being acquired and practised. That being said, an ideal performance should be effortless, as the technique of what is being executed is ingrained and stored in the subconscious. It is this unconscious competence that plays out in real world performance. It is possible to have control over the environment during practice, but a performance entails an element of stress, known as performance anxiety. Physiological stress is an integral part of any performance. It is when it assumes pathological proportions, that it casts a negative shadow over skills and thereby over the outcome as well. There is no way to rein in or harness all the stress inducing factors, but it is possible to reduce the undesirable impact they have on performance.

Mental readiness and its role in attaining excellence in surgical performance (74).

What are the mental factors that play a part in achieving excellence in surgical performance? To arrive at an answer to this question, highly proficient specialist surgeons from neurosurgery, cardiac, vascular, orthopaedic, plastic surgery and general practices were asked for their views and their methods of preparing for surgical procedures. Of the three key factors, mental, technical and physical, mental readiness was regarded as the most important for excellence in surgical performance. with a 49% vote. The technical and physical factors were allotted 41% and 10% of the votes respectively. It was mental readiness that made the biggest difference between good and bad surgical performance.

Positive imagery was an indispensable factor for mental readiness. The best performers followed a regimen, a series of activities to induce a positive state of mental readiness before their surgery. A good plan spells a clear sense of direction. A big majority, 73% to be precise, would anticipate the complications and also their solutions. 'What would I do if...?' is a pertinent question in devising plans to deal with the unknown. Verbalising potential complications, listing procedural steps and reviewing plans of action, is a good formula for success. Seven out of ten of the surgeons surveyed made sure they had enough time to be mentally prepared for the impending surgery. A quiet place and time to reflect on and formulate a plan and being focused were their mantras.

Pre-performance cognitive simulation: The mental practice of a well-learned skill prior to an actual performance can influence the motivational system, e.g. to reduce anxiety or boost self-confidence. It could even be used to modify the cognitive system by consolidating the accurate sequencing of a complex series of movements.

Cognitive simulation during performance: The imagery experience can no longer decoupled from the action itself. Rather, imagery is placed along a continuum extending from the overt movement to its mental representation. This has led to the belief that imagery could be performed not only before, or after, but also during the physical execution of the movement. It is beneficial for both, concentration and the anticipation of forthcoming events. Imagery therefore, is akin to action simulation, which involves the representation of the future and prospective judgements.

Post-performance cognitive simulation: To review the negative as well as positive aspects of the performance. The performer should be aware of what contributed a positive performance. Distinguishing the factors that lead to success and developing strategies to enhance performance in similar situations in the future will improve consistency. Imagery can be used to review previous peak performances, which will reinforce the belief that it can be done again, boosting confidence effectively.

J. Becoming familiar with unknown situations

At the elite levels of international sporting competitions, the venues are photographed for the benefit of competing athletes, who study photographs of the pools, fields, arenas, dressing rooms and even warm-up areas so that they can create effective images and see themselves performing there. This helps in familiarisation with the environment before the actual competition.

Similarly, surgeons too can visualise unfamiliar operating theatres where they will be performing in the future. A surgeon, who has been using cognitive simulation, visits five different hospitals a week to perform operations . He has successfully started using cognitive simulation to help him feel at ease in and adjust to the different operating theatres.

K. Practicing psychological skills

Athletes who can handle pressure, remain focused in spite of distractions and confident in the face of setbacks, are the ones who excel. Occasionally a surgeon may get frustrated by something that had happened before he arrives at the theatre or is distracted by theatre conditions, or he may frets over the anaesthetist's doings. All this can and does influence whether a surgical procedure will go ahead as smoothly as it should. A surgeon's job throws up problems constantly, both in the operation theatre and outside. Strategies are needed to cope with stressful situations, which are acquired through experience, or by trial and error rather than via formal training. Cognitive simulation can accelerate and enhance the strategy evolving process, by systematically developing appropriate techniques for specific occasions. The concept of mental skills training is new to surgery, but the importance of being able to cope with adversity has been known for a long time. Surgery involves performing both physically as well as mentally. Peak performance remains an unattainable dream unless a surgeon develops the psychological qualities marked by the four Cs: Commitment, Concentration, Confidence and Control.

Commitment

Cognitive simulation has both a cognitive as well as motivational function (158). Motivational imagery focuses on end results or goals to be achieved. Commitment involves developing motivational skills that encourage the performer to improve, even when immediate progress is not apparent. Without commitment, no challenging long-term goals can be achieved and performance enhancement will remain a dream.

Perhaps one of the intriguing aspect of imagery is, how it can focus a surgeon's resources toward the attainment of a specific goal. Specific goal imagery is like a self-fulfilling prophecy. The internal images that surgeons have of themselves tend to influence overt behaviour. A performer who sees himself 'choking' under pressure, will most likely do just that in a critical situation. However, a performer with successful images of himself will often emerge as a successful despite trouble and pressure. The formulation of a goal image activates the mind towards attaining it. Without a specific goal image the mind cannot focus on the resources needed to attain it.

Concentration

Concentration entails maintaining undiluted focus during performance, devoting attention to important task cues and responding quickly and correctly to any circumstance. Surgeons need to switch their attention during procedures to both broad and narrow foci, externally to environmental cues or internally to strategies. As with other skills, practice attending to various cues during training is essential to ensure that the focus is maintained during critical situations.

Mental readiness in surgeons and its role in excellence in surgical performance (77).

A surgeon is (or should be) in a completely focused state during performance. This focus is characterised by complete concentration (which is the 100% that all surgeons profess), the ability to anticipate the next stage (which 46% affirm), and being able to direct energy in a positive and focused way (which 46% claim). The fully focused state is accompanied by an absence of anxiety (which 79% attest to). The surgery takes on a life and rhythm of its own and is a connected, flowing and even enjoyable experience.

Imagery can be used to rehearse the focusing and refocusing of plans during a stressful procedure. In the case of a mistake or an unexpected turn of events, one can return to the proper task cues for appropriate implementation.

Confidence

In some aspects, confidence is a by-product of preparation for surgery. Self-confidence comes into being with the belief in success and in one's own competence. Confidence is enhanced by past success in a procedure and also imagining a successful completion. Whosoever believes in his mind that they can succeed, has greater chances of succeeding in the actual procedure. Replaying successful performances in your imagination will bring about positivity in one's ability to succeed. If observing another surgeon demonstrating the proper execution of a skill can enhance self-confidence, imagine what the imagery of you succeeding in the same skill could do!

Sports science suggests that coping imagery has a greater effect on self-confidence than mastery images. Mastery images involve imagining the perfect execution of a skill, while coping images involve imagining the overcoming of an obstacle or difficulty during performance and eventual success. The latter being closer to reality, coping images should be used firstly, and the mastery images in conclusion, to conjure up a perfect performance.

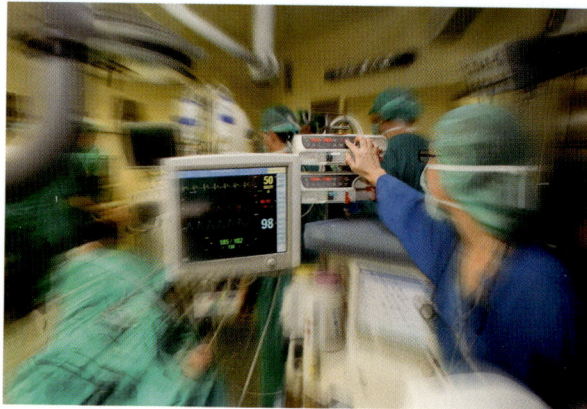

Imagery for stress control

Range of developments over last few years have brought about a significant rise in the levels of stress that surgeons experience. Surgeons constantly confront new challenges in the fulfilment of their responsibilities. Dealing with the difficulties of treating the critically ill means taking life or death decisions on a daily basis, which makes surgery synonymous with stress (159).

Even outside of the surgical domain, stress adversely affects performance (160). Although stress can catalyse performance, and for some surgeons, it is the reason for their fascination with surgery; extreme stress can have harmful consequences. For surgeons, undue stress prevails mostly in the operation theatre (161). A recent systematic review established that stress does harm surgical performance, most markedly in trainee surgeons (162). There is published research on the damaging impact of stress on surgeons.

In case of choosing a particular procedure, surgeons do not consider the risks of the procedure to themselves, rather they evaluate the advantages and disadvantages of procedures for the patient. Can a surgical technique pose hazards for surgeons? A study explored if surgeons suffer excessive mental strain during laparoscopic versus open sigmoid resection? (163) Endoscopic and other minimally invasive surgical techniques are known to benefit patients, but how stressful they are for surgeons is not known. It is a fact however that advanced minimally invasive surgery is far more challenging to perform. In this study, electrocardiograms of two surgeons who performed ten conventional and ten laparoscopic sigmoid sections, alternating as primary surgeon and assistant, were continuously recorded during the procedures. The main outcome measure was Heart Rate Variability (HRV). Measuring HRV is an accepted method of assessing mental strain, and is more sensitive than measuring heart rate alone. According to Czyzeska, HRV is the most reliable parameter in the measurement of mental load during surgery (164). The recordings showed that HRV was significantly higher for the laparoscopic procedure than during conventional surgery, and higher for the surgeon than the assistant. Indeed, performing laparoscopic colorectal surgery causes higher mental strain than performing conventional surgery.

Being more demanding, advanced laparoscopic surgery then may entail disadvantages for surgeons, and the risk of inadvertent events could increase if several procedures are undertaken in a day. Two or more prolonged procedures per day could result in mishaps during surgery owing to possible lapses in concentration. Minor mistakes that may be without consequences in conventional surgery can set off major complications in laparoscopic surgery.

A Swedish study stated that surgeons are at an increased risk of death from ischaemic heart disease than the general population (165). The major difference between the studied population was in regard to work characteristics. Surgeons work at a faster pace, their schedules are hectic, they are unable to relax after work, and their work is also physically demanding. The increase in sympathetic activity during surgery may have deleterious effects, ranging from worsening of ischaemia to lethal arrhythmias or sudden death. Laparoscopic procedures therefore do pose hazards for surgeons. Despite all this, surgeons for the most part are expected to dismiss the consequences of stress on their performance, than professionals in other similarly dynamic settings.

Besides occupational stresses, surgeons also encounter a range of stress inducing conditions while performing procedures. Severely ill patients, administrative work loads and less than ideal operation theatre conditions, can all add to the stress. The noise levels in some operation theatre are known to be as loud as 100 decibels, equal to that of a street market. These are harmful to the performance of complex procedures. All these stress-inducing situations often work in combination to burden the surgeon inexorably.

The effect of stress inducing conditions on the performance of a surgical procedure was gauged in a study (166).

Thirteen surgeons with different levels of experience did a laparoscopic procedure under five settings in five different groups.

1. A mathematical task
2. Operating theatre background noise of 80 decibels
3. Performance to be performed as quickly as possible
4. All three stressors combined
5. Quiet conditions

The effect of these conditions on performance was assessed by means of a motion analysis system and an error score. The results showed a substantial rise in the path length per movement of the right hand in the third group and there was a major rise in the path length per movement of the left hand in the first, third and fourth groups. A considerably greater number of errors were observed under all four stress-inducing conditions. The results highlighted that all three stressors led to compromised dexterity and increased the frequency of errors.

Experienced surgeons more often than not emphasise the positively demanding nature of surgical practice and reject that stress is problematic. However, ask them a question like, "How do they achieve being unruffled during crises or surgical complications?" and the answer will reveal that they manage to cope with it, and do not regard the high levels of stress as a problem. Some surgeons do acknowledge that stress is a vital feature in their day-to-day work and they are acutely aware of their innermost state during nerve-wracking situations. Stress can be useful and challenging, but excessive stress can and does induce errors.

A qualitative study (167) investigated stressors in surgery, their influence on performance and analysed the coping strategies surgeons adapt. Both, consultants and trainee surgeons were part of the survey. Wide-ranging arrays of intra-operative stressors were recognised during the interviews.

Sources of stress elucidated from the interviews :

Emergency cases
Surgical complications
Complex procedures
Equipment problems
Teamwork problems
Distractions
Personal factors

It was acknowledged by most surgeons that stress had both positive as well as negative effects. Senior surgeons showed a mindfulness of their actions, and they were capable of explaining coping strategies they used with clarity. Most of them applied those strategies intuitively, on 'automatic pilot' and hence did not feel stressors worsen their performance. Trainees stated comparable intra-operative stressors, but conveyed doubts about their own capacity and had disjointed, rather than refined coping strategies.

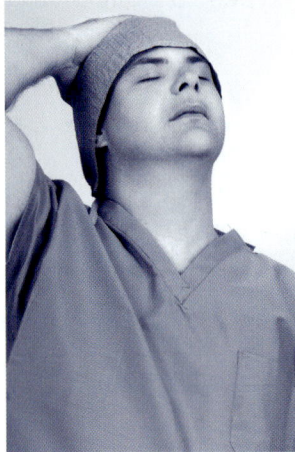

Coping skills for stressful conditions are not explicitly considered throughout surgical training, or discussed openly amongst associates. Most surgeons develop strategies by trial and error, or by watching seniors managing critical situations. The authors of this study concluded that stress substantially affects surgical performance,but surgeons are not taught in an organised manner about how to cope.

Another study (168) investigated the impact of stress and coping strategies on surgical performance while the surgeons performed on simulators. Thirty surgeons performed in a crisis and non-crisis scenario. Their stress levels were measured by various methods: self-assessment and observer ratings of stress; heart rate; heart rate variability and salivary cortisone. Coping strategies were evaluated qualitatively and were then converted to numerical score. Outcome measures of technical skills included objective structured assessment of technical skills (OSATS). The operative end result were assessed by end product assessment (EPA). The results showed that even in the non-crisis simulation, a higher coping score considerably improved EPA. Thus it showed that successful coping strategies were positively related to surgical performance. It highlighted that stress and coping skills are critical issues in the surgical outcome while managing the challenges.

The article described 5 types of effective coping strategies among surgeons

1. Preventive coping
planning the operation; checking instruments; team briefing
2. Anticipatory coping
Reducing inevitable stresses; anticipating problems and back-up planning; early recognition.
3. Proactive coping
Enhancing personal resources; mental rehearsal; broadening knowledge
4. Intra-operative coping
Self control: calming down, reducing own stress responses, self-talk, focusing
5. Control of the situation: stop and stand back technique, intra-operative prioritising

This study revealed surgeons' flexible approaches to manage stressful situations. The strategies enabled them to improve performance in extremely challenging conditions. Another revelation was that coping skills are independent of experience, highlighting that those skills are not necessarily acquired automatically during day-to-day work. This calls attention to the need for training in coping strategies to be incorporated into continued professional development. Despite the burning need for stress management training, novices gather how to deal with stress from their mentors casually at best, or by trial and error at worst. Can formal stress management training be helpful for surgeons?

Stress management training for surgeons –
A randomised, controlled, intervention study
Annals of Surgery. 2011 (169).

In a randomised control study, surgeons were randomly assigned to the intervention or control group. The intervention group was offered training on coping strategies and mental rehearsal. Performance outcomes were obtained during simulated procedures that comprised of objective structured assessment of technical skills and end product assessment rated by experts. Stress was assessed using questionnaires, observer rating, heart rate variability and salivary cortisol. The intervention group showed greater teamwork for surgical performance, increased coping skills and reduced stress. No significant changes were identified in the control group. The conclusion of the study was that the intervention had a positive effect on coping, stress, and non-technical skills during surgical procedure.

From the studies that have been discussed so far one would agree that it is conceivable to program an effective stress management agenda for surgeons.

Investigators from Imperial College, under the guidance of Professor Darzi, conducted another pioneering study using imagery techniques to investigate if mental practice reduced stress among surgeons (170).

A prospective, randomised controlled design included 20 surgeons enrolled by random sampling. After basic assessment, the surgeons were trained on an evidence-based virtual reality (VR) curriculum. After the training they were divided in to either mental practice or control groups. Each participant performed five VR laparoscopic cholecystectomies (LC). The imagery group carried out ½ hour of mental practice prior to performing the procedure. The control group was involved in an unconnected activity. Stress was measured subjectively by the validated State-Trait Anxiety-Inventory (STAI) questionnaire and objectively by a continuous heart rate (HR) monitor and salivary cortisol. The results showed that comparing the mental practice arm with the control arm, subjective stress (STAI) was lesser for the former. Also the objective stress was considerably decreased for the mental practice group in terms of the physiological parameters. Substantial negative associations were found in relation to stress and imagery, i.e. a higher imagery score was correlated to lower stress.

Given the fact that the subjective as well as objective results differed between the intervention and control groups, one can conclude that the mental practice intervention worked as a successful stress reduction approach. This inference echoes the conclusions in sports psychology that recommend that in addition to refining cognitive skills, mental practice helps in optimising psycho-physiological changes (171). The possible mechanisms underlying mental practice may be acting as a kind of 'stress inoculation training'. If this is the case, then the greater the imagery quality, the lower the subsequent stress. Substantial associations between cognitive simulation and stress imply that this to be the fact. Additionally, the meaningful relationships found among the three stress indices in this study validate this statement. It is the first such study to illustrate that cognitive simulation can reduce the psychological, neuro-endocrine and cardiovascular effects of stress.

Other than its indisputable effectiveness in this respect, cognitive simulation has the attraction of being economical and simple to implement, virtues that are invaluable in the current economic climate. Conclusively, incorporation of cognitive simulation into surgical practice will assist in reducing stress lastingly, and in minimising the chronic effects of stress.

Key points

■ Cognitive simulation perforce has a wide range of applications in
surgical practice that includes:

Acquiring skills

Shortening the learning curve

Maintaining the level of skill

Providing variety to practice

Transferring skills from an established technique

Hindering the decay of skills

Acquiring and practising strategies

Examining performance problems

Performance related use of Imagery

Becoming familiar with unknown situations

Practising psychological skills

To manage stress

Epilogue

'See one, do one, teach one' was the mantra of the era when I was a surgical trainee. However, looking back, it did not help me to cover the breadth of experience I needed to become skilled in the range of surgeries I performed later in my career. During my training, more than a decade ago, I spent a majority of working time dealing with clinical matters: examining patients, admitting them, and yes, performing operations. Over the years I have seen trainees getting less clinical experience. Surgical volume has decreased as less invasive procedures have replaced established procedures. If we take the decreased volume as a given, a smart approach is to get more out of each procedure.

The first laparoscopic cholecystectomy was performed in 1987. This landmark surgery paved the way for a change in the way operations are performed, and also in the way surgeons are trained. After the introduction of this minimal invasive surgery (MIS) it became apparent that surgeons needed to overcome some psychomotor hurdles in order to perform them successfully. The first hurdle was controlling the long instruments that passed through the skin portals. This meant that the surgeon received no tactile feedback. Also, instead of his own eyes, he had to rely on a pixilated image on a monitor that needed processing visual information, increasing a surgeon's cerebral work. The images from a single camera failed to provide binocular cues to judge the depth. Perhaps the most formidable obstacle was the apparent counter-intuitive movement of instruments. When the surgeon moved his hand wielding the instrument to the right, in the monitor it was seen moving to the left. This caused a proprioceptive-visual conflict. The use of MIS also meant the end of cutting opportunities provided by relatively straight forward surgical procedures such as open hernia repair, since they had now turned into advanced procedures requiring advanced training. The reduced working times and the changes, thanks to new approaches and technologies, added to the difficulties.

To address these issues, surgeons started attending short courses to get to grips with the new techniques. The training varied, ranging from an anesthetised pig in a fully equipped operating room, to an inanimate bench model. Training became available for a diverse and wide range of procedures but it became apparent that the benefits of these short courses had limitations. When the surgical establishment was facing these training problems, the development of surgical simulators paved the way for simulation to evolve from a concept to clinical validation.

Training on simulators is considered to be a novel method in surgery. As a matter of fact, it is not. Neither is virtual reality simulation, which is the most recent evolution. Surgery has used simulation type models for training that ranged from models of the human body to cadaveric dissections. The art of simulation has been known for some time, the only difference is, its science has made advances in the last few decades.

Surgical simulation has not been proven to be a silver bullet though. Cost is a significant prohibiting factor. The most sophisticated simulators cost millions, not to forget the maintenance cost. Such simulators run on highly sophisticated technology, which makes them fragile and expensive to run. Acquiring bad habits is a problem of poorly designed simulators. For example, some oesophagoscopy simulators recommend the surgeon to pass the endoscope straight down past the vocal cords into the oesophagus. However, with real patients, navigating the endoscope past the vocal cords is rarely straight forward and a patient would be at risk if a surgeon were to carry out this simulation method. Proponents of simulation technology boast about the advantages of fidelity of the recent simulators. What they don't tell you is, the higher the fidelity, the higher the price. Besides, until recently, surgeons were trained on the highest fidelity model possible, i.e. real patients; nonetheless some failed to learn. Why was this, if simulator fidelity correlated with skill acquisition? On the top of that, some surgeons do not seem to know what to look for in the simulation fidelity. In that case, a high definition video recording of surgical procedure is not of much use other than showing what they should do during a procedure. Those who are hyperbolical about the use of simulators ought to pay heed to this lament by T. S. Eliot - "where is the knowledge we have lost in information?" Surrounded by state of art in technological wizardry, we have got carried away by what is technically possible and have forgotten about the real task at hand is!

The real task is creating an appropriate sensory experience and a deliberate practice. Ericsson has shown that performance excellence is not something that individuals are born with, but is something that is acquired by deliberate practice. Deliberate practice is more than repeated experience and is not just about working harder. People who engage in deliberate practice look at areas of improvement and then set about creating a plan which will take them beyond their current abilities. It involves many of the factors that we have discussed in this book. When applied by motivated individuals, this is an effective process for gaining expertise. Cognitive simulation incorporates the principles of deliberate practice with the specific aim of improving surgical skills. An understanding of human cognition, psychomotor learning and how they impinge on the skilled performance has helped to develop the concept of cognitive simulation. Thus, here is an opportunity that will benefit the field of surgery well into the future.

In many ways, surgical performance is similar to the competitive sports performance. Both require intense concentration and complex fine and gross motor abilities. Both are routinely performed under considerable pressure. Preparation for a surgical procedure, much like preparation for a sports performance, involves both the cognitive and motivational aspects. Given these similarities, surgeons would benefit from adopting the techniques that have been proven to improve psychomotor performance in sports. No doubt, the aim for surgeons is not to win a competition, as it is for athletes, but rather to be competent in every procedure performed.

Once a renowned golfer Gary Player was on a golf course where a gentleman saw him putting the ball in a hole in a single stroke. The gentleman came to Gary and said, "You got 50 bucks if you knock the next one in." Gary holed the next one in. The gentleman said, "You got 100 bucks if you hole the next one." In it went for the third time in a row. The gentleman said, " I have never seen anyone so lucky in my life." Gary shot back, "Well, the harder I practise, the luckier I get!"

He had a similar message to convey, when Louie Pasteur said "Chance favors the prepared mind." Napoleon Bonaparte and General Patton were both known to indulge in role playing. Both of them were able to cope with almost any situation, thanks to their mental preparation. Similarly, incorporating mental skills training into surgical curriculums could teach surgeons at an early stage how to maximise its benefits, improving acquisition and retention of skills.

Although simulation technology is becoming accepted as a training strategy, studies have shown that cognitive simulation can be an effective adjunct to this "technical simulation." By using the "simulation center in the mind", surgeons will need to spend less time and money in the simulation laboratory. Ironically, the human mind cannot tell the difference between a real and imagined experience. The same building of neural pathways occurs by imagining practice as it does by actual practice. Mental practice is almost, if not as effective, as real practice. In fact, most practices include some imagined component as the situations which you practice are rarely the same as those in which you will ultimately perform. It is not that we should necessarily worry about doing mental practice instead of real practice, as both give similar results, but rather, we should include the mental component in our real practice. In view of evidence that mental practice combined with physical practice results in better skill acquisition than that from either of them alone, mental practice could be used as an adjunct to physical training (172). Of course, cognitive simulation will not replace physical practice altogether but it must be borne in mind that this is available to all and is a much less resource intensive approach, since it is free of cost!

As operative interventions becomes less and less invasive for more and more procedures, how are surgeons are expected to retain their skills for open procedures that are common today but will become infrequent in the near future? As the minimally invasive technologies are implemented, we should not forget that if something goes wrong, it is going to be a surgeon performing an open procedure, who will have to pick up the pieces. Without any possibility of an open surgical simulator being available within the next decade, surgeons need a built-in process to address this issue. Cognitive simulation is an ideal technique to fulfill that role.

So how can we use cognitive simulation to improve our practice? You have taken the first step by going through the material provided in this book. I assume that you have a fair understanding of the art and science of using cognitive simulation to enhance performance, and also when and where to use it. The next step would be to incorporate its use into day to day practice to prepare for upcoming cases. Whether in a quiet place some where in the operating suite or even in a coffee room or at a later stage, while scrubbing for the procedure. It can also be used to acquire strategic thinking: for example, a trainer and trainee cognitively simulate a procedure together and then discuss, might bring up contingency strategies used by experienced surgeons that will be made explicit to the trainee.

A word of caution though. Although cognitive simulation is not difficult to acquire, it should not be trivialised as 'just closing the eyes and thinking about the steps of the operation. Advantage of cognitive simulation over other types of mental practice, for example visualisation, is in the principal governing learning: the learning is enhanced to the degree where the conditions of practice are similar to those of actual performance. If we consider the degree of similarity, then just thinking about making an action is only slightly similar to the actual action while cognitively simulating an action would be far more similar than that. Thus using cognitive simulation would be closest to actually making the action and not just 'going over the steps of the operation in your mind'.

Learning cognitive simulation can be equated to learning a foreign language. Just as it would involve constant learning and efforts before one can read and understand a foreign language newspaper, likewise, cognitive simulation will require practice before one attains fluency. Proficient surgeons are good at what they do because of their attention to small details. For example, it may not make a lot of difference when suturing a wound, if all the knots are placed on one side of the wound, if the distance between them is equal and the suture tails are of same length. However, it is the attention to these kind of details that characterise the attitude of an expert surgeon. Similar attention to details will be required from someone who wants to get the best results out of cognitive simulation.

Finally, I would like to say that there's nothing to stop a motivated surgeon, the sky and the imagination are the only limits for those willing to take the plunge into the emerging and splendor domain of cognitive simulation!

References

1.   Cosman PH Cregan PC Martin CJ Cartmill JA. Virtual reality simulators: Current status in acquisition and assessment of surgical skills. *ANZ Journal of Surgery.* 2002;72 (1): 30-34.

2.   Mahmood S Anwar S Ahmed J Tayyab M O'Regan D. A survey of UK surgical trainees and trainers: latest reforms well understood but perceived detrimental to surgical training. *Surgeon.* 2012; 10 (1): 9-15.

3.   Hamdorf JM Hall JC. Acquiring Surgical Skills. *British Journal of Surgery.* 2000; 87 (1): 28-37.

4.   Bosk C. *Forgive and Remember: Managing Medical Failure.* University of Chicago, Chicago; 1979.k

5.   Gawande A. Creating the educated surgeon in the 21st century. *American Journal of Surgery.* 2001;181 (6): 551–556.

6.   Bridges M Diamond D. The financial impact of teaching surgical residents in operating room. *The American Journal of Surgery.* 1999;177 (1): 28-32.

7.   Cuschieri A. Whither minimal excess surgery: tribulations and expectations. *American Journal of Surgery.* 1995;169 (1): 9-19.

8.   Wong JA Matsumoto ED. Primer: cognitive motor learning for teaching surgical skill—how are surgical skills taught and assessed? *Nature Reviews Urology.* 2008;5: 47-54.

9.   McDougall E. Validation of Surgical Simulators. *Journal of Endourology*. 2007;21 (3): 244-247.

10.   da Cruz JA Sandy NS Passerotti CC Nguyen H Antunes AA Dos Reis ST Dall'Oglio MF Duarte RJ Srougi M. Does training laparoscopic skills in a virtual reality simulator improve surgical performance? *Journal of Endourology*. 2010; 24 (11): 1845-9.

11.   Strom P Kjellin A Hedman L Wredmark T Fellander-Tsai L. Training in tasks with different visual-spatial components does not improve virtual arthroscopy performance. *Surgical endoscopy and other interventional techniques.* 2004;18 (1): 115-20.

12.   Prabhu A Smith W Yurko Y Acker C Stefanidis D. Increased stress levels may explain the incomplete transfer of simulator-acquired skill to the operating room. *Surgery.* 2010;147 (5): 640-45.

13.   Korndorffer Jr JR Dunne JB Sierra R Stefanidis D Touchard CL Scott DJ. Simulator training for laparoscopy suturing using performance goals translates to the operating room. *Journal of American College of Surgeons.* 2005;201 (1): 23-9.

14.   Palter VN Orzech N Aggarwal R Okrainec A Grantcharov TP. Resident perceptions of advanced laparoscopic skill training. *Surgical Endoscopy.* 2010;24 (11): 2830-2834.

15.   .Kneebone, R. Practice, rehearsal and performance: an Approach for Simulation-based Surgical and Procedure Training. *Journal of the American Medical Association.* 2009;302 (12): 1336-7.

16.   Gladwell M. *The physical genius*. The New Yorker. August 2, 1999.

17.   Rosser JC Lynch PJ Cuddihy L Gentile DA Klonsky J Merrell R. The Impact of Video games on Training Surgeons in the 21st Century. *Archives of Surgery.* 2007;142 (2): 181–186.

18.   Schlickum MK Hedman L Enochsson L Kjellin A Felländer-Tsai L. Systematic Video Game Training in Surgical Novices Improves Performance in Virtual Reality Endoscopic Surgical Simulators: A Prospective Randomized Study. *World Journal of Surgery.* 2009;33 (11): 2360-2367.

19.   Murray CJL Lopez AD. Mortality by cause for 8 regions of the world: global burden of disease study. *Lancet.* 1997;349 (9061): 1269-76.

20.   Way LW Stewart L Gantert W Liu K Lee CM Whang K Hunter JG. Causes and prevention of laproscopic bile duct injury-analysis of 252 cases from a human factors and cognitive psychology perspective. *Annals of surgery.* 2003;237 (4): 460-469.

21.   Hugh T. New Strategies to Prevent Laparoscopic Bile Duct Injury – Surgeons can learn from Pilots. *Surgery.* 2002;132 (5): 826-835.

22.   Sodergren MH Orihuela-Espina F Froghi F Clark J Teare J Yang GZ Darzi A. Value of orientation training in laparoscopic cholecystectomy. *British Journal of Surgery.* 2011;98 (10): 1437-1445.

23.   Scott TM Hameed SM Evans DC Simons RK Sidhu RS. Objective assessment of surgical decision making in trauma after a laboratory based course: durability of cognitive skills. *American Journal of Surgery.* 2008;195 (5): 599–602.

24.   Orlick T Partington J. Mental links to excellence. *The Sports Psychologist.* 1988;2: 105-130.

25.   Maxwell JP Masters RSW Eves FF. From novice to no know-how. A longitudinal study of implicit motor learning. *Journal of Sport Science.* 2000;18 (2): 111-120.

26.   Hardy L Mullen R Jones G. Knowledge and conscious control of motor actions under stress. *British Journal of Psychology.* 1996;87 (4): 621-636.

27.   Kopta J. An approach to the evaluation of operative skills. *Surgery.* 1971;70 (2): 297-303.

28.   Lippert FG Spolek GA Kirkpatrick GS Briggs KA Clawson DK. A psychomotor skills course for orthopedic residents. *Journal of Medical Education.* 1975;50 (10): 1982-1983.

29.   Pearce AJ Thickbroom GW Byrnes ML Mastaglia FL. Functional reorganization of the corticomotor projection to the hand in skilled racquet players. *Experimental brain research.* 2000;130: 238-243.

30.   Leff DR Leong JJH Aggarwal R Yang G-Z Darzi A. Could Variations in Technical Skills Acquisition in Surgery Be Explained by Differences in Cortical Plasticity? *Annals of Surgery.* 2008;247 (3): 540 –543.

31.   Lacourse MG Orr ELR Cramer SC Cohen MJ. Brain activation during execution and motor imagery of novel and skilled sequential hand movements. *Neuroimage.* 2005;27 (3): 505-519.

32.   Kohl RM Roenker DL. Bilateral transfer as a function of mental imagery. *Journal of Motor Behaviour.* 1980;12 (3): 197-206.

33.   Shuell, T. Phases of meaningful learning. *Review of Educational Research.* 1990;60 (4): 531-547.

34.   Raman, M Donnon T. Procedural skills education – colonoscopy as a model. *Canadian Journal of Gastroenterology.* 2008;22 (9): 767-770.

35.   Zheng B Cassera MA Martinec DV Spaun GO Swanstrom LL. Measuring mental workload during the performance of advanced laparoscopic tasks. *Surgical Endoscopy.* 2010;24 (1): 45-50.

36.   Pernar LIM Pernar LI Ashley SW Smink DS Zinner MJ Peyre SE. Master Surgeons' Operative Teaching Philosophies: A Qualitative Analysis of Parallels to Learning Theory. *Journal of Surgical Education.* 2012;69 (4): 493-8.

37.   Hunter JG Sackier JM. *Minimally invasive surgery.* New York, McGraw-Hill.Inc; 1993.

38.Cauraugh JH Martin M Martin KK. Modeling Surgical Expertise for Motor Skill Acquisition. *The American Journal of Surgery.* 1999;177 (4): 331-336.

39.   Feil PH Reed T Hart JK. Continuous knowledge of results and psychomotor skill acquisition. *Journal of Dental Education.* 1986;50 (6): 300-303.

40.   Schmidt R. A schema theory of discrete motor skill learning. *Psychology Review.* 1975;82 (4): 225-260.

41.   DesCôteaux JG Leclère H. Learning surgical technical skills. *Canadian Journal of Surgery.* 1995;38 (1): 33-38.

42.   Schueneman AL Pickleman J Freeark RJ. Age, gender, lateral dominance, and prediction of operative skill among general surgery residents. *Surgery.* 1985;98 (3): 506-514.

43.   Wanzel KR Hamstra SJ Anastakis DJ Matsumoto ED Cusimano MD. Effect of visual-spatial ability on learning of spatially complex surgical skills. *Lancet.* 2002;359 (9302): 2310-2311.

44.   Wanzel, KR Anastakis DJ McAndrews MP Grober ED Sidhu RS Taylor K Mikulis DJ Hamstra SJ. Visual-Spatial Ability and FMRI Cortical Activation in Surgery Residents. *American Journal of Surgery.* 2007;193 (4): 507-510.

45.   Squire D Giachino AA Profitt AW Heaney C. Objective comparison of manual dexterity in physicians and surgeons. *Journal of Canadian Surgery.* 1989;32 (6): 467-470.

46.   Risucci D Geiss A Gellman L Pinard B Rosser JC. Experience and visual perception in resident acquisition of laparoscopic skills. Current *Surgery.* 2000;57(4): 368-372.

47.   Luursema J-M Buzink SN Verwey WB Jakimowicz JJ. Visuo-spatial ability in colonoscopy simulator training. *Advances in Health Science Education Theory and Practice.* 2010;15 (5): 685-694.

48.   Eyal R Tendick F. Spatial ability and learning the use of an angled laparoscope in a virtual environment. *Studies in Health Technology Information.* 2001;81: 146-152.

49.   Abernathy CM Hamm RM. *Surgical Intuition.* Philadelphia, Hanley & Belfus, chapter 10;1995.

50.   Murdoch JR Bainbridge LC Fisher SG Webster MHC. Can a simple test of visual-motor skill predict the performance of microsurgeons? *Journal of the Royal College of Surgeons Edinburgh.* 1994;39 (3): 150-152.

51.   Keehner M Lippa Y Montello DR Tendick F Hegarty M. Learning a Spatial Skill for Surgery: How the contributions of abilities change with practice. *Applied Cognitive Psychology.* 2006;20 (4): 487-503.

52.   Cauraugh JH Martin M Martin KK. Modeling Surgical Expertise for Motor Skill Acquisition. *American Journal of Surgery.* 1999;177 (4): 331-336.

53.   Ashford D Bennett SJ Davids K. Observational modelling effects for movement dynamics and movement outcome measures across differing task constraints: a meta-analysis. *Journal of Motor Behaviour.* 2006;38 (3): 185-205.

54.   Rizzolatti G Fadiga L Matelli M Bettinardi V Paulesu E Perani D Fazio F. Localization of grasp representation in humans by PET: 1. Observation versus Execution. *Experimental Brain Research.* 1996;111 (2): 246-252.

55.   Ram N Riggs SM Skaling S Landers DM McCullagh P. A comparison of modelling and imagery in the acquisition and retention of motor skills. *Journal of Sports Sciences.* 2007;25 (5): 587-597.

56.   Decety J Grèzes J Costes N Perani D Jeannerod M Procyk E Grassi F Fazio F. Brain activity during observation of actions. Influence of action content and subject's strategy. *Brain.* 1997;120 (10): 1763-1777.

57.   Galton F. *Hereditary Genius: An inquiry into its laws and consequences.* 1979 edition. London: Julian Freidman; 1869.

58.   Ericsson K. The Scientific Study of Expert Level of Performance: General Implications for Optimal Learning and Creativity. *High Ability Studies.* 1998;9 (1): 75-100.

59.   Howe MJA Davidson JW Sloboda JA. Innate Talents: Reality or Myth? *Behavioral and Brain Sciences.* 1998;21 (3): 399-407.

60.   Schrag D Panageas KS Riedel E Cramer LD Guillem JG Bach PB Begg CB. Hospital and Surgeon Procedure Volume as Predictors of Outcome following Rectal Cancer Resection. *Annals of Surgery.* 2002;236 (5): 583-592.

61.   Cowan JA Dimick JB Thompson BG Stanley JC Upchurch GR. Surgeon volume as an indicator of outcomes after carotid endarterectomy: an effect independent of specialty practice and hospital volume. *Journal of American College of Surgeons.* 2002;195 (6): 814-21.

62.   Begg CB Riedel ER Bach PB Kattan MW Schrag D Warren JL Scardino PT. Variations in morbidity after radical prostatectomy. *New England Journal of Medicine.* 2002;346:1138-44.

63.   Ericsson KA Krampe RT Tesch-Romer C. The role of deliberate practice in the acquisition of expert performance. *Psychological Review.* 1993;100 (3): 363-406.

64.   Ericsson K. Deliberate Practice and the Acquisition and Maintenance of Expert Performance in Medicine and Related Domains. *Academic Medicine.* 2004;79 (10): 70-81.

65.   Ericsson KA - chapter 38, The influence of experience and deliberate practice on the development of superior expert performance. In: *The Cambridge Handbook of Expertise and Expert Performance.* Cambridge University Press. 2006. Page 685 -706.

66.   Abernethy B Poolton JM Masters RS Patil NG. Implications of an expertise model for surgical skills training. *ANZ Journal of Surgery.* 2008;78 (12): 1092-1095.

67.   Whiting HTA Vereijken B. The acquisition of coordination in skill learning. *International Journal of Sport Psychology.* 1993;24 (4): 343-57.

68.   Sakurai S Ohtsuki T. Muscle activity and accuracy of performance of the smash stroke in badminton with reference to skill and practice. *Journal of Sport Science*. 2000;18 (11): 901-914.

69.   Gallagher AG Richie K McClure N McGuigan J. Objective psychomotor skills assessment of experienced, junior, and novice laparoscopists with virtual reality. *World Journal of Surgery*. 2001;25 (11): 1478-1483.

70.   Kahol K Leyba MJ Deka M Deka V Mayes S Smith M Ferrara JJ Panchanathan S. Effect of fatigue on psychomotor and cognitive skills. *American Journal of Surgery*. 2008;195 (2): 195-204.

71.   Rosenberg A. The surgeon skill set in minimally invasive total knee arthroplasty. *American Journal of Orthopaedics*. 2006;35 (7 Supplement): 30-2.

72.   Riscucci D. Visual-Spatial Perception and Surgical Competence. *The American Journal of Surgery*. 2002;184: 291-295.

73.   Abernathy CM Hamm RM. *Surgical secrets*. Hanley & Belfus. 102 -142;1994.

74.   McDonald J Orlick T Letts M. Mental readiness in surgeons and its links to performance excellence in surgery. *Paediatrics Orthopaedeics*. 1995; 15: 691-697

75.   Woolfolk RL Murphy SM Gottesfeld D Aitken D. Effect of mental rehearsal of task motor activity and mental depiction of task outcome on motor skill performance. *Journal of Sport Psychology*. 1985;7(2): 191-197.

76.   Hall C. Imagery in sport and exercise. In: Hausenblas H Janelle C Singa R (eds.) *Handbook of research on sports psychology*. 2nd ed. New York, Wiley; 2001. p. 529-549.

77.   DeFrancesco C Burke KL. Performance enhancement strategies used in a professional tennis tournament. *International Journal of Sport Psychology.* 1997;28(2): 185-195.

78.   Lloyd, Paul J.; Foster, Sandra L. Creating healthy, high-performance workplaces: Strategies from health and sports psychology. *Consulting Psychology Journal: Practice and Research,* Vol 58(1), 2006, 23-39.

79.   Nicklaus J. *Golf My Way.* New York: Simon and Schuster; 1974. page79.

80.   Orlick T Partington.J. Excellence through mental training. *Sport Psychology Bulletin.* 1986; 69- 75.

81.   Martin K Murphy S. The use of imagery in sport. In: Horn TS (ed.) *Advances in Sport Psychology.* 2nd ed. Champaign, Illinois: Human Kinetics; 2002. p 405-439.

82.   Morris T Spittle M. Examination of internal and external imagery of open and closed sports skill using concurrent verbalization. In: presented at *Australian Psychological Society annual conference.* Melbourne, Australia; September, 1998.

83.   Eton D Gilner FH Munz DC. The measurement of imagery vividness. A test of the reliability and validity of the vividness of visual imagery questionnaire and the vividness of movement imagery questionnaire. *Journal of Mental Imagery.* 1998;22 (3&4): 125-136.

84.   Callery P Morris T. Imagery, self efficacy, and goal kicking performance. In: Lidor, R. and M Bar-Eli, M. (eds.) *International society of sport psychology – IX world congress of sport psychology.* Tel Aviv, Ministry of Education, Culture and Sport. 1997. p. 109-177.

85.   Lesgold A. Problem solving. In: Sternberg RJ (ed.) *The Psychology of Human Thought.* Cambridge University Press: New York; 1988. p 203.

86.   Washburn M. *Movement and Mental Imagery.* Boston:Houghton; 1916.

87.   Hale B. The Effect of Internal and External Imagery on Muscular and Ocular Concomitants. *Journal of Sport and Exercise Psychology.* 1982;4 (4): 379–387.

88.   Suinn R. Body Thinking: Psychology for Olympic Champions. In: Suinn R. *Psychology in Sports: Methods and Applications.* Minneapolis: Burgess; 1980. p 306–315.

89.   Sackett RS. Movement imagination. *The Journal of General Psychology.* 1934;10 (2): 376 -398.

90.   Kohl RM, Roenker DL. Mechanism Involvement during Skill Imagery. *Journal of Motor Behavior.* 1983;15 (2): 179-190.

91.   Feltz DL, Landers DM. The Effects of Mental Practice on Motor Skill Learning and Performance: A meta-analysis. *Journal of Sport Psychology.* 1983;5(1): 25-57.

92.   Driskell JE, Copper C, Moran A. Does mental practice enhance performance? *Journal of Applied Psychology.* 1994;79 (4): 481-492.

93.   Decety J. The neurological basis of motor imagery. *Behavioural Brain Research.* 1996;77: (1-2): 45-52.

94.   Jeannerod M. The Representing Brain: Neural correlates of motor intention and imagery. *Behavioural and Brain Sciences.* 1994;17 (2): 187-202.

95.   Kosslyn SM Alpert NM Thompson WL Maljkovic V Weise SB Chabris CF Hamilton SE Rauch SL Buonanno FS. Visual mental imagery activates topographically organized visual cortex: PET investigations. *Journal of Cognitive Neuroscience.* 1993;55 (3): 263-287.

96.   Deecke L. Planning, preparation, execution, and imagery of volitional action. *Cognitive Brain Research.* 1996;3 (2): 59-64.

97.   Cunnington R, Iansek R ,Bradshaw JL ,Phillips JG. Movement related potentials associated with movement preparation and motor imagery. *Experimental Brain Research.* 1996;111: 429-436.

98.   Rodionov V, Zislin J, Elidan J. Imagination of body rotation can induce eye movements. *Acta Otolaryngology.* 2004;124 (6): 684-689.

99.   Tremayne P, Barry R. Elite pistol shooters: Physiological patterning of best versus worst shots. *International Journal of Psychophysiology.* 2001;41 (1): 19-29.

100.   Deschaumes-Molinaro C Dittmar A Vernet-Maury E. Relationship between mental imagery and sporting performance. *Behavioural Brain Research.* 1991;45 (1): 29-36.

101.   Bakker M, de Lange FP Helmich RC Scheeringa R Bloem BR Toni I. Cerebral correlates of motor imagery of normal and precision gait. *Neuroimage.* 2008;41 (3): 998-1010.

102.   Decety J Jeannerod M. Mentally simulated movements in virtual reality: Does Fitts' law hold in motor imagery? *Behavioral Brain Research.* 1996;72 (1): 127-34.

103.   Paivio A. Coding distinctions and repetition effect in memory. In: Bower, G. (ed.) *Psychology of Learning of Motivation.* Volume 9. New York: Academic press; 1975.

104.   Paivio A. *Mental representations: A dual coding approach.* New York: Oxford University Press; 1986.

105.   Grouios G. Mental Practice: Review. *Journal of Sport Behavior.* 1992;50 (1): 42-59.

106.   Page SJ Sine W Nordell K. The effects of imagery on female college swimmers' perception of anxiety. *The Sport Psychologist.* 1999;13 (4): 458-469.

107.   McAuley E. Modeling and Self Efficacy: A test of Bandura's model. *Journal of Sports Psychology.* 1985;7 (3): 283-295.

108.   McKenzie AD Howe BL The effect of imagery on self efficacy for a motor skill. *International Journal of Sport Psychology.* 1997;28 (2): 196-210.

109.   Dennis M. Visual imagery and the use of mental practice in the development of motor skills. *Canadian Journal of Applied Sport Sciences.* 1985;10, 4S–16S.

110.   Richardson A. Mental Practice: A Review and Discussion, part one. *Research Quarterly.* 1967;38, 95–107.

111.   Weinberg R. The relationship between mental preparation strategies and motor performance: A review and critique. *Quest.* 1982;33 (2): 195–213.

112.   Durand M Hall C Haslam IR. The effects of combining mental and physical practice on motor skill acquisition. *The Hong Kong Journal of Sports Medicine and Sports Science.* 1997;4, 36-41.

113.   Pascual-Leone A Nguyet D Cohen LG Brasil-Neto JP Cammarota A Hallett M Modulation of muscle responses evoked by transcranial magnetic stimulation during the acquisition of new fine motor skills. *Journal of Neurophysiology.* 1995;74 (3): 1037-43.

114.   Roure R Collet C Deschaumes-Molinaro C Delhomme G Dettmar A Vernet-Maury E. Imagery quality estimated by autonomic response is correlated to sporting performance enhancement. *Physiology and Behavior.* 1999;66 (1): 63-72.

115.   Behrmann M. The Mind's Eye Mapped onto the Brain's Matter. *Current Directions in Psychological Science.* 2000;9 (2): 50-4.

116.   Kosslyn SM Thompson WL Alpert NM. Neural Systems Shared by Visual Imagery and Visual Perception: A Positron Emission Tomography Study. *Neuroimage.* 1997;6 (4): 320-34.

117.   Sharma N Pomeroy VM Baron JC. Motor imagery: A backdoor to the motor system after stroke? *Stroke.* 2006;37 (7): 1941-1952.

118.   de Vries S Mulder T. Motor imagery and stroke rehabilitation - a critical discussion. *Journal of Rehabilitation Medicine.* 2007;39 (1): 5-13.

119.   Braun SM Beurskens AJ Borm PJ Schack T Wade DT. The effects of mental practice in stroke rehabilitation: a systematic review. *Arch Phys Med Rehabil.* 2006;87(6): 842–852.

120.   Kosslyn SM Thompson WL Ganis G. *The Case for Mental Imagery.* New York: Oxford University Press; 2006.

121.   Kosslyn SM Thompson WL. When is early visual cortex activated during visual mental imagery? *Psychological Bulletin.* 2003;129(5): 723-746.

122.   Sanders CW Sadoski M Bramson R Wiprud R Van Walsum K. Comparing the effects of physical practice and mental imagery rehearsal on learning basic surgical skills by medical students. *American Journal of Obstetrics and Gynecology.* 2004;191 (5): 1811-1814.

123.   Sanders CW Sadoski M Van Walsum K Bramson R Wiprud R Fossum TW. Learning basic surgical skills with mental imagery: using the simulation centre in the mind. *Medical education.* 2008;42 (6): 607-612.

124.   Immenroth M Buerger T Brenner J Nagelschmidt M Eberspaecher H Troidl H. Mental training in surgical education - randomized control trial. *Annals of Surgery.* 2007;245 (3): 385-395.

125.   Arora S Aggarwal R Sevdalis N Moran A Sirimanna P Kneebone R Darzi A. Development and validation of mental practice as a training strategy for laparoscopic surgery. *Surgical Endoscopy.* 2010;24 (1): 179-187.

126.   Arora S Aggarwal R Sirimanna P Moran A Grantcharov T Kneebone R Sevdalis N Darzi A. Mental Practice Enhances Surgical Technical Skills, A Randomized Controlled Study. *Annals of Surgery.* 2011;253 (2):265–270.

127.   Hall C. Measuring imagery abilities and imagery use. In: Duda J (ed.) *Advances in sport and exercise psychology measurement.* Morgan Town, West Virginia: Fitness Information Technology; 1998. p.165-172.

128.   Guillot A Collet C Dittmar A. Relationship between visual versus kinesthetic imagery, field dependence-independence and complex motor skills. *Journal of Psychophysiology.* 2004;18 (4): 190-198.

129.   Vadocz EA Hall CR Moritz SE. The relationship between competitive anxiety and imagery use. *Journal of Applied Sport Psychology.* 1997;9 (2): 241-53.

130.   Zacks JM. Neuroimaging studies of mental rotation: A meta-analysis and review. *Journal of Cognitive Neuroscience.* 2008;20 (1): 1-19.

131.   Robin N Dominique L Toussaint L Blandin Y Guillot A Le Her M. Effects of motor imagery training on returning serve accuracy in tennis: the role of imagery ability. *International Journal of Sport and Exercise Psychology.* 2007;5 (2): 177-188.

132.   Vadocz EA Hall CR Moritz SE. The relationship between competitive anxiety and imagery use. *Journal of Applied Sport Psychology.* 1997;9 (2): 241-253.

133.   Martin K Murphy S. The use of imagery in sport. In: Horn, T. (ed.) *Advances in sports psychology.* 2nd ed. Champaign, Illinois: Human Kinetics; 2002. p. 405–439.

134.   Cocude M Mellet E Denis M. Visual and mental exploration of visuo-spatial configurations: Behavioral and neuroimaging approaches. *Psychological Research.* 1999;62 (2-3): 93-106.

135.   Lotze L Montoya P Erb M Huelsman E Flor H Klose U Birbaumer N Grodd W. Activation of cortical and cerebellar motor areas during executed and imagined hand movement: an fMRI study. *Journal of Cognitive Neuroscience.* 1999;11 (5): 491-501.

136.   Cui X Jeter CB Yang D Montague PR Eagleman DM. Vividness of mental imagery: Individual variability can be measured objectively. *Vision Research.* 2007;47 (4): 474–478.

137.   Schmidt RA Wrisberg CA. *Motor learning and performance: A problem-based learning approach.* (Third ed.) Champaign, Illinois, Human Kinetics; 2004.

138. Jacobson E. Electrical measurements of neuromuscular states during mental activities. *American Journal of physiology.* 1930;91:567–606.

139. Isaac A. Mental Practice – Does it work in the field? *Sport Psychologist.* 1992;6:192 – 198.

140. Rodgers W Hall C Buckolz E. The effect of an imagery training program on imagery ability, imagery use, and skating performance. *Journal of Applied Sport Psychology.* 1991;3 (2): 109 – 125.

141. Newell FN Ernst MO Tjan BS Buelthoff HH. Viewpoint dependence in visual and haptic object recognition. *Psychological Science.* 2001;12 (1): 37-42.

142. Kosslyn SM Ball TM Reiser BJ. Visual images preserve metric spatial information: Evidenced from studies of image scanning. Journal of *Experimental Psychology: Human Perception and Performance.* 1978;4 (1): 47-60.

143. Louis M Guillot A Maton S Doyon J Collet C. Effect of imagined movement speed on subsequent motor performance. *Journal of Motor Behavior.* 2008;40 (2): 117-32.

144. Hall C. Imagery for movement. *Journal of Human Movement Studies.* 1980;6, 252 – 264.

145. Hall JC. Imagery practice and the development of surgical skills. *American Journal of Surgery.* 2002;184 (5): 465-470.

146. Debarnot U Creveaux T Collet C Gemignani A Massarelli R Doyon J Guillot A. Sleep related improvements in motor learning following mental practice. *Brain and Cognition.* 2009;69 (2): 389-405.

147.   Jolly B. Clinical logbooks: recording clinical experiences may not be enough. *Medical Education.* 1999; 33 (2): 86-88.

148.   Hopper AN Jamison MH Lewis WG. Learning curves in surgical practice. *Postgraduate Medical Journal.* 2007;83: 777-779.

149.   Meinke AK Kossuth T. What is the learning curve for laparoscopic appendectomy? *Surgical Endoscopy.* 1994; 8 (5): 371-375.

150.   Tekkis PP Fazio VW Lavery IC Remzi FH Senagore AJ Wu JS Strong SA Poloneicki JD Hull TL Church JM. Evaluation of learning curve in ileal pouch-anal anastomotis surgery. *Annals of Surgery.* 2005;241 (2): 262-268.

151.   Parikh D Johnson M Chagla L Lowe D McCulloch P. D2 gastrectomy: Lessons from a prospective audit of the learning curve. *British Journal of Surgery.* 1996;83 (11): 1595-1599.

152.   Sutton DN Wayman J Griffin SM. Learning curve for oesophageal cancer surgery. *British Journal of Surgery.* 1998;85 (10): 1399-402.

153.   Hopper AN Jamison MH Lewis WG. Learning curves in surgical practice. *Postgraduate Medical Journal.* 2007;83: 777-779.

154.   Blasier RB. The Problem of the Aging Surgeon. *Clinical Orthopaedics and Related Research.* 2009;467 (2): 402-411.

155.   Neumayer LA Gawande AA Wang J Giobbie-Hurder A Itani KMF Fitzgibbons RJ Reda D Jonasson O. Proficiency of surgeons in inguinal hernia repair. Effect of experience and age. *Annals of Surgery.* 2005;242 (3): 344-352.

156.   Heck DA Robinson RL Partridge CM Lubitz R Freund D. Patient outcomes after knee replacement. *Clinical Orthopaedic and Related Research.* 1998;356: 93-110.

157.   Gould G Monsaingeon B. *No, I am not at all eccentric.* [Non, je ne suis pas du tout un excentrique]. Paris: Fayard 1986.

158.   Paivio A. Cognitive and motivational functions of imagery in human performance. *Canadian Journal of Applied Sport Sciences.* 1985; 10: 22S–28S.

159.   Sevdalis N Forrest D Undre S Darzi A Vincent C. Annoyances, disruptions, and interruptions in surgery: the Disruptions in Surgery Index (DiSI). *World Journal of Surgery.* 2008;32 (8): 1643–1650.

160.   Vedhara K Hyde J Gilchrist ID Tytherleigh M Plummer S. Acute stress, memory, attention and cortisol. *Psychoneuroendocrinology.* 2000;25: 535–549.

161.   Arora S Hull L Sevdalis N Tierney T Nestel D Woloshynowych M Darzi A Kneebone RL. Factors compromising safety in surgery: stressful events in the operating room. *American Journal of Surgery.* 2010;199 (1): 60–65.

162.   Arora S Sevdalis N Nestel D Woloshynowych M Darzi A Kneebone RL. The impact of stress on surgical performance: a systematic review of the literature. *Surgery.* 2010;147 (3): 318–330.

163.   Boehm B Roetting N Schwenk W Grebe S Mansmann U. A Prospective Randomized Trial on Heart-rate Variability of the Surgical Team during Laparoscopic and Convention Sigmoid Resection. *Archives of Surgery.* 2001;136 (3): 205-210.

164.   Czyzewska E Kiczka K Czarnecki A Pokinko P. The surgeon's mental load during decision making at various stages of operation. *European Journal of Applied Physiology.* 1983: 51: 441-446.

165. Arnetz BB Andreasson S Strandberg M Eneroth P Kallner A. Comparison between surgeons and general practitioners with respect to cardiovascular and psychological risk factors among physicians. *Scandinavian Journal of Work and Environmental Health*. 1988;14 (2): 118-124.

166. Moorthy K Munz Y Dosis A Bann S Darzi A. The effect of stress inducing conditions on the performance of laparoscopy task. *Surgical Endoscopy*. 2003;17 (9): 1481-84.

167. Wetzel CM Kneebone RL Woloshynowych M Nestel D Moorthy K Kidd J Darzi A. The Effect of Stress on Surgical Performance. *The American Journal of Surgery*. 2006;191 (1): 5-10.

168. Wetzel CM Black SA Hanna GB Athanasiou T Kneebone RL Nestel D Wolf JHN Woloshynowych M. The Effect of Stress and Coping on Surgical Performance During Simulations. *Annals of Surgery*. 2012;251 (1): 171-176.

169. Wetzel CM Akram G Hanna GB Athanasiou T Black SA Kneebone RL Nestel D Woloshynowych M. Stress Management Training for Surgeons – A randomized, controlled, intervention study. *Annals of Surgery*. 2011;253 (3): 488-494.

170. Arora S Aggarwal R Moran A Sirimanna P Crochet P Kneebone RL Sevdalis N Darzi A. Mental Practice: Effective Stress Management Training for Novice Surgeons. *Journal of American College of Surgeons*. 2011;212 (2): 225–233.

171. Moran A. Cognitive psychology in sport: Progress and prospects. *Psychology of sport and exercise*. 2009;10 (4):420–426.

172. Arora S. Surgeons in training may benefit from mental visualisation. *British Medical Journal*. 2013;346: e8611 Published 7 January 2013.

Appendix

Cognitive simulation script

This script contains the tasks of the laparoscopic cholecystectomy with sensory cues. These sensory cues are colour coded– Blue, red, amber, green and purple. You are expected to do what the color represents

Blue - call up a detailed picture in your mind. (Visual modality)

Red - experience what you might say. (Verbal modality)

Grey - experience what you might hear. (Auditory modality)

Green - feel the action. (Kinesthetic modality)

Purple - Feel the touch. (Tactile modality)

1. Positioning and preparation

Imagine entering the operating theatre,
where you see the anaesthetist, the patient on the table and rest of the team.
You go over the WHO checklist with the patient confirming the procedure.
As the patient is anaesthetised, you confirm with the nursing staff that appropriate equipment is available for surgery.
You position patient appropriately for surgery.
You scrub up and

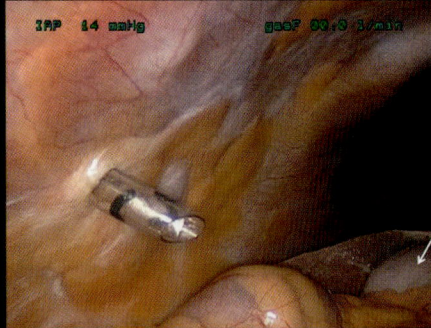

Laparoscopy and insertion of working ports

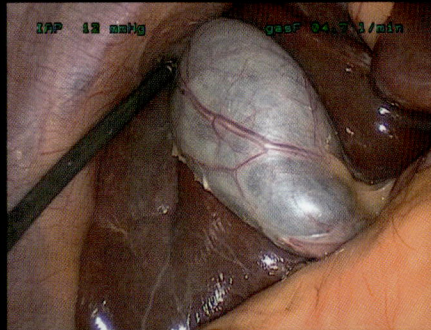

Gall bladder

Gall bladder fundus pushed up by assistant

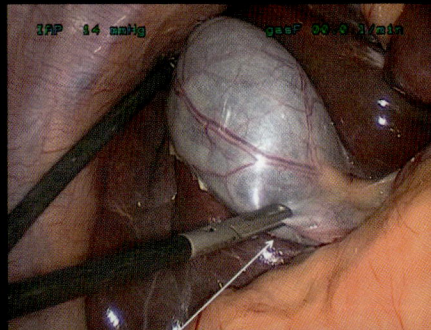

Hartmann's pouch grasped and pulled down and out

wear a sterile gown and gloves.

You clean the abdomen,

drape the sterile area.

You ask the anaesthetist if it is okay to start.

She replies "yes, please go ahead".

2. Create a pneumoperitoneum

You ask the scrub nurse for local anaesthetic and knife.

You inject 5 ml local anaesthetic in the infra-umbilical skin.

You then stretch the skin with your left hand downwards

and firmly press the knife transversely for about 2 cm.

You ask the assistant to retract

the yellow soft fatty tissues to see the white sheath.

You incise the sheath with knife. You push the assistants' retractor through the sheath opening.

You see the pearly white peritoneum bulge through the sheath opening.

You open this with scissors between forceps, insert your index finger to sweep around

and feel the smooth surface of the peritoneum free of any adhesions.

You then insert the 10 mm port for camera and attach the CO_2 insufflation tubing to the port.

As the insufflation proceeds you feel and

see the abdomen distend gradually.

Once the abdomen is tense,

you insert the camera through the port.

You look all around the abdomen. You look at the glistening normal bowel and absence of bleeding. You look towards the gall bladder and liver.

You then tell the anaesthetist "please tilt the head end of table up to about 30 degrees and towards me about the same".

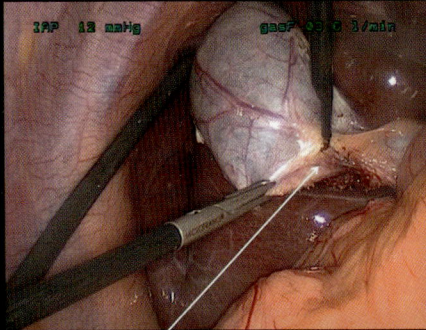

Cutting peritoneum on right side

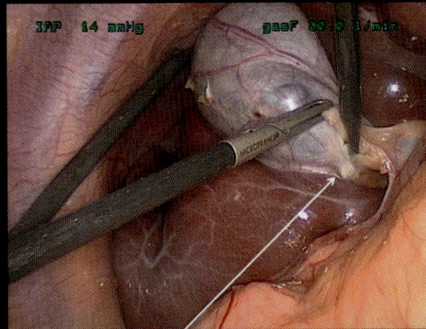

Cutting peritoneum on left side

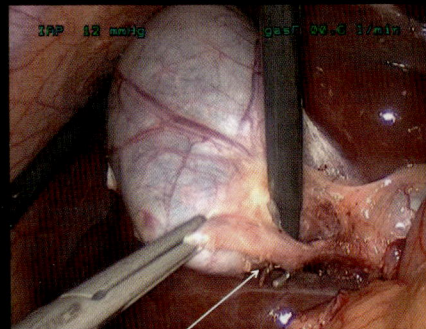

Isolating cystic duct junction with gall bladder

3. Insert laparoscopic ports

You tell the assistant to hold camera asking him to keep what you are doing in the centre of the screen

You feel the inverted V of the sterno-costal margin

and decide the site of the epigastric port under lower edge of liver by looking from inside while pressing your index finger from the outside.

You incise the skin with knife about 5 mm. You then take the 5 mm port from the nurse.

You arm the port by pressing the arming switch, which clicks in place.

You place the port at the 5 mm incision and push with a slow twisting movement through the abdominal wall,

whilst watching from the inside.

You feel the tissues give way as the port tip emerges inside the peritoneal cavity.

As the final resistance of the last layer gives way you hear the click as the port disarms.

You then similarly insert two more 5 mm ports 4 finger-breadths below costal margin on the right (middle and lateral ports) - one in the anterior axillary line and the last one about an inch medial.

4. Perform laparoscopy and retract gall bladder

You insert one atraumatic grasper from epigastric port and one from middle port on right. You lift up liver and

look at the gall bladder. It is bluish-grey color and distended.

You use the toothed gall bladder grasper through the lateral most port to hold the fundus of the gall bladder. You push it upwards and laterally,

feeling the springy resistance of the liver.

You ask the assistant, to hold the grasper so that the gall bladder is retracted up.

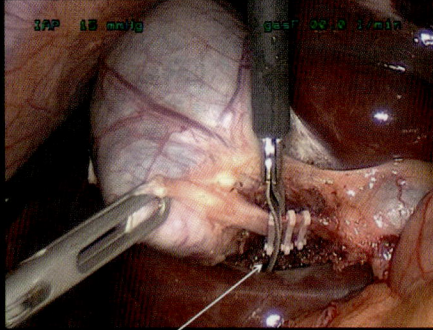

Dividing cystic duct between clips

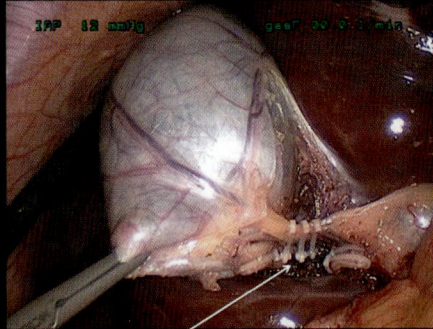

Clips applied on cystic artery

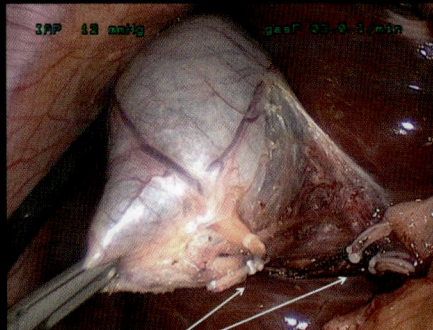

Divided cystic duct and artery

5. Expose Calot's triangle

You insert an atraumatic grasper from the middle port and firmly grasp the Hartmann's pouch and retract it downwards,
feeling it stretch the tissues.
You insert a diathermy hook through the epigastric port , press the diathermy paddle, burn with the back at junction between gall bladder and the fat of Calot's triangle.
As you do, you hear the buzzing noise
You see the tissue whiten with the coagulation burn and a bit of smoke.
You push the hook into this spot and lift up the tissue
feeling the resistance of the stretched strands.
You cut the stretched tissue. You carry on cutting the peritoneum near the gall bladder on the right side.
You the lift up the Hartman's pouch and with hook incise the peritoneum on the left of the gall bladder. You can now pull out the gall bladder out of it's liver bed easily and
see the stretched tissues in the Calot's triangle area.

6. Dissect and expose Cystic artery and Cystic duct

You dissect near the Hartmann' pouch, using the hook, teasing strands of tissue away from gall bladder.
You see junction of the gall bladder and pearly white cystic duct. Superiorly you see the cystic artery as whitish red structure with the rounded pinkish lymph gland sitting on it. You dissect around the artery to separate it out.
You confirm the safety of this Calot's triangle dissection by seeing the cystic duct, cystic artery and the gall bladder clealy lifted away from liver.

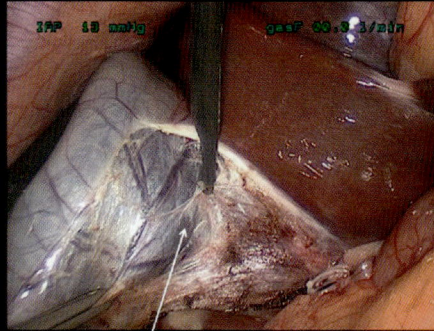

Releasing the gall bladder from the liver

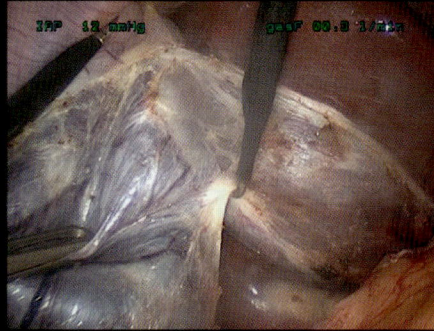

Smoke of burning tissue causing haziness of field

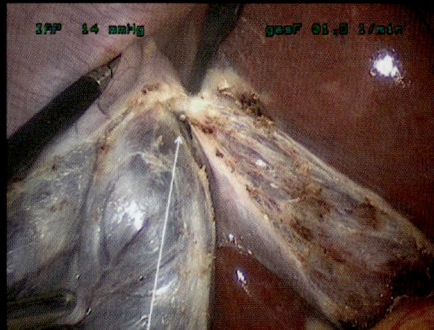

Dividing the last attachment of gall bladder to liver

7. Clip and cut the Cystic Duct and Artery

You insert a 5 mm clip applicator through the epigastric port. You place the open jaws of the applicator around the cystic duct and close it till you feel the snap of the clip engaging. You apply total two clips on patient's side and one on gall bladder side. You then take laparoscopic scissors, insert through the epigastric port and cut the cystic duct leaving two clips on patient's side. You then similarly apply three clips on the artery and cut between with scissors, leaving two clips on patients side.

You see the gall bladder spring away from the liver.

8. Dissect gallbladder off liver bed

You inspect the cut cystic duct and cystic artery. This does not reveal leaking bile or bleeding.

You hold gall bladder with your atraumatic grapers using your left hand and stretch it away from the liver. You use the diathermy hook with your right hand to release the strands by coagulating them.

As the smoke of burning tissues accumulates you see it as increasing haziness of the visual field.

You open the valve of the lateral port to release the gas.

You see the gall bladder released gradually from its bed. Before the last strand is cut, you inspect the gall bladder bed and see that there is no bleeding.

9. Extract the dissected gallbladder

You remove your left hand grasper and grasp the retriever bag with it.

Your assistant then removes the camera.

You insert the bag through the camera port with its tail hanging out.

Your assistant re-inserts the camera.

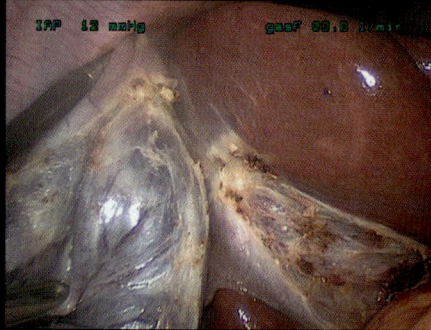

Gall bladder fully separated from liver

Retrieval bag/pouch inserted

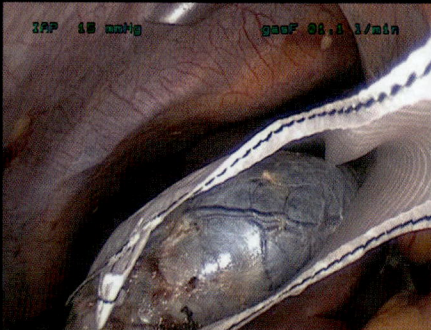

Gall bladder specimen put in the retrieval bag

Using the grasper with your right hand you insert it through the epigastric port. With the grasper you hold the edge of the bag and open it.
The assistant, holding the gall bladder fundus, pushes it into the open bag. You see that the gall bladder is in the bag. You do a final inspection of the gall badder bed and
then pull the tail of the bag gradually.
Your assistant removes the camera and you pull the port and bag out slowly through the wound.

10. Final Check and irrigation, close up patient

You re-insert the port through the infra-umbilical site and insert the camera.
You inspect the area of surgery. You see everything is dry.
You remove rest of the ports asking the assistant to observe the inside openings.
You then remove camera and the camera port.
You tell the anaesthetist "please straighten the patient".
Your assistant then retracts the infra-umbilical incision using two right angle retractors.
You stitch the sheath opening and then close the skin with sub-cuticular suture.